Hits, Clicks and Misses:
The Traffic Exchange Experience

By Jon Olson

ISBN: 978-1-4303-1576-6

For my son Matthew – You are the reason I work so hard! It's a blessing and joy to watch you grow up!

Introduction

It's amazing what can happen when you have a dream. I was never good at working for someone else. I've got to be the world's worst employee. I'm not sure if it was my upbringing, or my dislike of authority. Every time I had to go to work when I was a teenager, I cringed. It was never for me. That's why, when I first saw the opportunity to earn a living on the Internet, I did not walk, I ran at the opportunity with arms wide open. Eight years later...

In my years of working with traffic exchanges, I have seen a lot of trends come and go, but something has remained the same. That same desire and dream that each surfer has when they start a session of surfing. They dream of a more fulfilling life. A chance to sit back, and enjoy the fruits of their labor. The dream of working for yourself. It's very empowering. Surfing a traffic exchange has never been glorious, and at times, it can be downright boring. However, the people that make up this industry all have a few things in common.

Desire, passion, vision and 'the dream'. Sure, everyone's path will be different, but the end result is what we are all 'clicking' for. The traffic exchanges are one of the most effective form of free advertising online for good reason, they work. They work because the people work. Without people, this business model would crumble. Without dreams, passions, desire and vision, we would be all spinning our wheels aimlessly. While we, as an industry, continue to grow and mature, we can look back at our achievements, and our failures and learn from them.

This is who this book is dedicated to, this is who I wrote this book for. The Traffic Exchange Surfer! No matter what anyone tells you, believe me when I say, you are the reason this industry works.

If you have ever read an issue of Hit Exchange News, you will know my motto well, *75% numbers and 25% opinion!* Well, for this book we'll change it up a bit. It will be *75% experience and 25% opinion.* Welcome to Traffic Exchanges: Hits, Clicks and Misses!

The book you are reading is a collection of my experiences and thoughts for the past 3-plus years of writing Hit Exchange News – the first and only weekly traffic exchange publication. Going back over the years, I chuckle at some of the things I wrote (I am not the world's greatest author) and I hope you enjoy the trip down memory lane as well. There are some very good tips and tricks that you can use to your advantage if you are surfing in the traffic exchanges today. The book also has some short blurbs on the history of the exchanges and a brief overview of the wonderful world of the exchanges.

I thank you very much for joining me on an adventure in 'clicking'!

The History of the Traffic Exchange

Before I get into the first ever traffic exchange that was created, let me share with you a story about how I came face to face with these incredible little programs. It was back in 1999. I was a 'starving artist' in every sense of the word. While living in Toronto, Canada, I was busy at work, trying to make a name for myself in the music business. I was an artist manager of a very popular musical act, and even though the money was barely creeping in, we were heading in the right direction.

I was looking for a way to develop and promote the artists on the web. Somehow, I knew we needed an online presence of some sort. Now this was 1999, so the dot com boom was just getting 'ready to bust', but it was still new technology for many aspiring artists. By fluke or by chance, I came across this little program, while surfing, called AllAdvantage.com. This was one of the first 'Paid-2-Surf' programs on the net and it worked like this.

The All Advantage surf bar would be downloaded onto your computer. And once you opened the program, banners would be rotated in front of you. The 'surf bar' docked itself under your browser and you got paid for every hour that this thing rotated banners in front of you. Pretty neat, huh? I thought so and so did tens of thousands of other surfers. Before you knew it, All Advantage spawned dozens upon dozens of clone sites, all paying their members different amounts per hour for 'watching' banner ads. Remember, this was 1999. Banners were 'the' way to advertise online.

How much money did I make? Oh it was peanuts, but the thought of making any type of money on the Internet, simply by surfing absolutely blew me away. At its peak, All Advantage was paying its members up to 50 cents per hour for having the surf bar active. And there was more than just All Advantage. Names like Spedia, GoToWorld, Desktop

Dollars and countless others, all popped onto the scene to try to grab some of this perceived advertising revenue. Companies were paying to have their banner ad rotated on each of these system's surf bars and more and more Paid-2-Surf's kept popping up.

Eventually, advertisers got wise to the fact no one was looking at their banner ads, and the Paid-2-Surf bars became less effective for advertising dollars. However, it was just the beginning of the 'Paid-2-Surf' industry....And even today we are seeing a new breed of these programs start to 'pop up', pardon the pun.

The Paid-2-Surf Explosion

With the slow down of the Paid-2-Surf ad bars came the birth of a new service. The Paid-2-Read companies started to come online where members got paid for reading e-mails that got sent to your inbox. Imagine, earning 15 cents for reading an e-mail! It was pure bliss! But the secret to these programs' success was not the fact that you could earn 15 cents per email, the real benefit was the fact that each of these Paid-2 companies paid on multi-levels. Yes, the MLM structure had invaded the Internet and its first target were these free to join Paid-2 companies. So not only did you earn the 15 cents for clicking on an ad in your inbox, but you also got paid for referring new members to the program.

The concept of referring your friends and family, and get them to earn money by reading emails was huge. To this day, the Paid-2 industry is as popular as ever. The companies have come and gone, but the deal remains the same. Click on links in your inbox, make money. Refer new members, make even more money.

This was great! I've told my friends and family that I can make some extra bucks by reading emails, but where else can I promote these Paid-2 companies? This is the

Internet, I must be able to find places to advertise these great new services? What to do, what to do?

In The Beginning, There Was One...

I'm not sure if Michael Griffith knew what was about to happen when he started the web site called ClickThru.net. I'm really not even sure if he meant for his invention to promote these Paid-2 programs.

ClickThru.net was the first 'web site traffic exchange'. The term 'Banner Exchange' had existed before this, but this was new, this was entire web sites being 'exchanged' not just banner advertisements. The concept was extremely simple, I look at your web site, you look at mine. A timer would count down from 30 seconds, and then I was allowed to view the next site in the queue. The original business model actually cost members a buck a month, but this was soon dropped for the 'free to join' version. Click Thru was a huge success. For the first time ever online, a web site could guarantee web site owners the opportunity to exchange traffic with other site owners. Full page view exchanging and this was co-operative advertising at its finest. I scratch your back, you scratch mine. Check my site out, I'll look at yours and so on.

This program came out before there was ever any such thing as a 'pop up' or exit advertisement. Yes, the first traffic exchange was actually created the same year that Larry and Sergey decided the world needed more Google! Click Thru was ahead of its time and the members loved it. And what about the sites that people could view? There were musical artists, promoting their MP3.com homepage. There were family tree web sites. There were recipe sites where Grandma had her newest recipe for muffins. It was an amazing program. Different sites and different people in a brand new technology. And it grew...

When you strip everything away from Click Thru, you will again see co-operative advertising. The general idea behind the program was that it was becoming very hard to get good search engine rankings. This again was when Google first got its start and Yahoo ruled the search world. Web site owners did not have a place to get guaranteed page views, without paying a small fortune. The first ever traffic exchange filled a void and supplied a growing niche with the perfect place to advertise their web sites. Simply insert your site into the system and visit other web sites. For every web site you viewed, you would receive a page view in return. A very simple, but effective concept. Like I said, it grew!

When I joined Click Thru in 1999, I forgot what I came online for in the first place. I originally booted up my computer to promote my artists on the Internet. Well, after I discovered the Paid-2 programs, my priorities changed dramatically. So the first program I promoted in Click Thru was this crazy thing called zWallet (I hear some readers laughing already). Think Hotmail or gMail, but a service that paid you to send and receive mail. It was a fun concept, but I never did make that fortune I thought I would with it. Anyways, back to Click Thru. So the first program I promoted in the exchange was in fact, a Paid-2 program. Why? Simple, I wanted to build my downline. And build it I did. At the end of the year, I had around 1500 people in my downline at zWallet and this was all from my time surfing in ClickThru.net. I was hooked!

Time passed and before you knew it, a few new programs started to pop up that promised the same things as Click Thru, but had different names and different designs. Say hello to Hit Harvester, No More Hits, EZ Hits 4 U, and I Love Clicks. The traffic exchange industry was born and it all started from Mr. Griffith's vision. Thanks must go in order for the Grandfather of the Traffic Exchanges, his vision and creation is now responsible for millions of dollars in advertising every year. To this day, Click Thru is still a stellar program that has always done things a little differently than most exchanges. Its unique 'remote control' surfing console is a refreshing change from the regular surf bars that populate the exchanges. If you really want an eye opener, check out the Way Back Machine's history of Click Thru throughout its history. It even got rid of the dot net domain extension and now has the dot com.

The T.E. Terminology

Now that you have an overview of how these programs got their start, I think it's very important that we go over some terminology that is prevalent in the traffic exchanges. I will be referring to quite a few of these throughout the book, so take your time and go over this a few times. It will help you better understand what makes these programs 'click'.

Credits – Basically the 'currency' of the exchanges. Credits are exchanged within the program for page views, which results in people seeing your web site. All things being equal, one credit would normally equal one page view. So you can either surf for credits, buy credits or exchange credits. This is the life blood of a traffic exchange, the meat of how they work. Without proper credit management, a traffic exchange collapses.

Surf ratio – This describes the ratio in which surfers must view sites in order to receive a page view in return. For example, Click Thru was a 1:1 ratio, which meant that for every page view you looked at, you received a page view to your web site. The industry average, however, is a 2:1 ratio, meaning you must view 2 sites, to get 1 hit to yours. There are many different ratios from 3:1, to 5:1, to a 5:4 to a 3:2. Each exchange may have a different surf ratio.

Surf Bar – A traffic exchange basically has two frames within a web browser. The first frame would hold the member's web site, and the second frame would be the surf bar. The surf bar would contain information about the surf session. For example, it could read how many page views you have visited, or how many hits you have received. It also could house a spot for a banner advertisement, as well as spots for text link ads. Each exchange would have different surf bars, but almost all contain a timer that counts down the time remaining before you could view the next site.

Referral Levels – Most traffic exchanges, though not all, operate on a referral system. Meaning, they are multi-leveled in most cases, but the majority of them do reward you for introducing new members to the program. Some referral levels and bonuses are extremely unique, one can be found at TS25.com, which rewards you not for referring people, but for how active you are in the system itself. Some exchanges will develop many levels of referral bonuses with each level contributing to the member's total traffic earned. So not only do you receive page views for surfing the exchange, by referring new members, you can grow your traffic as well. This is not to be confused with MLM, whereas there is money being passed through each level. In fact, the exchanges have taken away the money earning on multi-levels and inserted 'traffic earnings'. Please note, the most powerful traffic exchanges are not 'money makers', but rather web advertising services.

Sign Up Bonuses – In some cases, traffic exchanges will actually reward you for signing up to their program immediately. For example, you may join XYZ Exchange and receive a sign up bonus of 50 credits (page views). This is basically a 'thank you' from the exchange owner for joining his / her program.

Multi Tabbed Browsers – They are quickly becoming the 'norm' online with programs such as Firefox and Internet Explorer 7. Basically, they are simply a web browser that allows you to open multiple 'tabs' in one window. So for example, let's say you wanted to open Amazon, eBay and Google all at once. Instead of opening three separate web browsers, you simply open a multi tabbed browser and load each site you want to view into its own tab. This practice has grown commonplace in the exchanges, as surfers do not limit their surfing to one exchange at a time. Good or bad, that has yet to be determined, but they exist, with or without the traffic exchanges.

H.E.N. - This stands for Hit Exchange News, which is my weekly e-zine that I have published since 2003. It's been called the pulse of the traffic exchange industry, and is read by thousands of surfers and exchange owners every week. We call it 'HEN' for short.

N.M.F. - This stands for Net Marketing Forum, which is the popular marketing forum that most traffic exchange users and surfers frequent daily. It's become quite the cornerstone of everything I do online, and is responsible for the majority of my network. Many successful joint ventures have been launched directly from the networking that takes place in this active community.

I.L.H. - IloveHits.com is one of the most popular traffic exchanges online and one of two that I own myself. With a membership of over 70,000 surfers, it continues to grow by the hundreds every week.

Hit Exchange – Just another way of saying traffic exchange. They are called start page exchanges, click through programs, visitors exchanges, as well as traffic exchanges. Different ways of saying it, same fun little programs!

Hits, Clicks and Misses

Note: This is a collection of articles from 3-plus years of Hit Exchange News. These are my thoughts, on paper and online from the weekly in's and out's of the traffic exchange industry. You will notice sometimes I'm a happy soul, and then the next week, I'm ranting about something else. That's the fun part of my job and I wouldn't change it for the world. I hope you enjoy the up's and down's of 3-plus years of surfing in the traffic exchanges.

Issue 45 – In The Beginning...

At the last count, there was something like 800 hit exchanges on the Internet. I'm sure that number can be higher, but for active programs, it may even be less. I'm not sure exactly, but one thing's certain, there are too many hit exchanges. The supply and demand of the exchanges is way out of synch. The number of ACTIVE users within these programs is not as high as some of us would like to think.

Does this mean the industry is failing? Nope, not by a long shot. There needs to be things done to improve the overall quality of hit exchanges, and steps are being put in place. Each owner has their own view of how things should run, and the diversity of each program is really what can shape the exchanges for years to come. New themes, new technology, new designs, new promotions, it's all adding substance to the industry.

What does the surfer do? Surfers are being asked to surf more, they do. They are asked to promote more, they do. I've got a question for the surfers now, what should we do? Limit our surfing to only a handful of exchanges, each day? Or continue to juggle exchange after exchange and, like I do almost daily, start to get inactive accounts because we just simply forget about a program?

It's a tough question, but something that I'm sure everyone has already decided. I've got my bookmarks, and those are the exchanges I choose to surf. It's a big list, because I need to TRY to be active in as many exchanges as I can, but I do limit my surfing to the programs that deliver what they promise.

Yes, we should limit our surfing to the programs that are actually delivering the hits, and it's important for owners to realize that surfers' time is money! For owners, providing a quality product is how you keep surfers coming back and spending their time (and money) in your program. I guarantee more exchanges will be released and many more will go offline. I myself choose quality over quantity any day!

Issue 46 – Pre Launch This!

Here's a term many of us have heard before... the ever popular 'marketing' term, the pre-launch. I noticed a few of these 'launches' over the past week and they struck my attention because I always ask myself, are they really needed? Or are they just a way for program owners to up sell you on something they plan to offer later?

Pre-launch is hype, nothing more. What it should be used for is to iron out any weaknesses in the scripts, or touch ups to the design. Instead, (in my opinion of course) they create hype within the online world, and the whole Internet will be knocking at the doors of these great money-making extravaganzas.

To put the term loosely...*LOL*.

This industry fails because of these fly-by-night operations that just seem to be promoted to no end before they officially launch, and then poof, they disappear without a trace within the next few weeks. Why? What scares people away? Is it the product itself? The program? Why does pre-launch almost GUARANTEE a program will fail. Want a good example? Here's one... Spam Terminator.

If owners used the pre-launch to actually build a solid foundation for these programs instead of filling people's minds with hype and hoopla, I would bet there would be a lot more 'success' in the online world. I've always said, more substance, less hype... My opinion on this is as follows... If something says 'pre-launch', don't even bother counting down from 10!

Issue 50 – The Golden Rule

Traffic exchanges operate on this golden rule, traffic must be exchanged. Without traffic flow, these programs simply do not work. You have to have people surfing the programs for the exchange to 'look good' on paper. And for the hit exchange owners, the better the traffic flow, the better chance they have to sell credits.

Selling credits, this is how exchange owners pay their server bills and continue to provide us with their program. Over the past week, there has been some discussion in the Net Marketing Forum about re-selling the traffic from the surfers. Basically when this happens, the hit exchange owner is denied profit from those credits.

On the other hand, those are credits that needed to be 'moved' anyway, and the more traffic that is flowing, the better the exchange can perform. So where does this leave us? Should hit exchange users definitely pay for all traffic directly from the exchange itself? Or are those credits, earned by surfers through either surfing or referral commissions, allowed to be used however the surfer sees fit?

You may draw your own conclusions because, believe me, this is a very divided topic. I think exchange credits should be sold by the exchange owners. I run a co-op and buy all my hits from the owners of the programs and I know how hard it is to make real income running a hit exchange.

Yes, exchange owners should profit from all traffic purchases, but the fact is that traffic will sell no matter what limitations we put on it. I guess it's an ethical issue, one which may never have a definitive answer, but here's hoping owners and surfers can prosper from traffic sales and traffic flow!

Here are some of the best hit exchanges to buy hits from, not only for quality, but for price as well! Cash Clicking, Traffic Meet, EasyHits4U, ClicksMatrix, Traffic Roundup, Mystical Maze, and Wolf Surfer. This is just a small list, but if you are thinking of buying hits at good prices and high quality, these are definitely some of the best programs to do so!

Issue 51 – Stop Clicking!

Don't click any more! Don't lift a single finger until those hits start being delivered! Yes folks, I'm taking a stand, I will not click in any single program that;

1. Offers over 200 credits to sign up!
2. Offers 1000s of credits to refer someone.
3. Or that has hundreds of credits that NEVER move out of my account.

Why the stance? Simple, if you want me to spend my valuable time in your program, you better be delivering what I'm there for, the hits. And if you are not delivering hits, there's no point in me clicking, is there?

To this day, it blows my mind why people insist on offering hundreds of credits to sign up, when no one has even surfed a single site yet. Folks, it's really a simple equation. You visit my site, I visit your site. This equation seems to have been 'complicated' for many exchange owners over time, but that's the main reason you have no traffic flow.

We (the surfers) are using your program to get hits to our site and to view other sites. Hey, I have no problem at all viewing hundreds of sites a day, but at least send me back a hundred hits or so. So to all the subscribers of H.E.N., I say let's concentrate our efforts (and time) on the hit exchanges that deliver what they promise.

Issue 51 – The Rotators!

Ever since I can remember, the rotator has been a part of the hit exchange industry. Think way back to the 'glory days' of E-Biz Rotator, it was everywhere. Guaranteed, the next site you viewed would be inserted into an E-Biz Rotator. Whether it be poor management or better products, the granddaddy of site rotators has fallen off stride. As that has happened, the question has been brought up many times, should hit exchanges still allow the use of rotators?

Rotators are being abused. Whether it's the insertion of a frame breaker, or the addition of a surfing URL, it's getting harder and harder to control and manage these programs. Let's face it, hit exchange owners have been left to not only police their hit exchange, but to police the rotators as well. It's not fair for the owner, and it's not fair for the surfer. Site rotators are such an important tool, though, and something has to be done to keep them in the exchanges.

I use my rotator about 7000 times each day, and professionally could not do without it. Something I've noticed over the past few months is that some hit exchange owners do not allow rotators in their programs, but offer them as tools for their members. A good chunk of the hit exchanges using the PHP Lite script are looking to ban site rotators, but still offer them to their members. Something is not right with that decision, but that seems to be the state of the industry.

So what can be done? Page Swirl has been working hard to make their program very 'exchange friendly' by launching a tool for exchange owners to view each and every site within the rotator. This is a great start and I know more is being done, but it's time for every rotator site out there to step up to the plate and scan each and every URL that is placed in their database. It's a must that they not allow frame breakers and bad URLs into the mix. A lot of work? Yes, but it's work that the exchange owners and surfers should not have to deal with.

Again, I'm a big fan of site rotators and use them each and every day. I'm hoping that those glory days can come back and site rotators are once again embraced by the exchanges!

Issue 52 – Too Many Features?

Traffic flow. It's what makes or breaks a hit exchange. If your members are not coming to surf, and returning to surf, your traffic will not get delivered. Exchange owners have tried everything from flash arcade games, contests, surfing games, trivia, mazes, to random draws. Every day, it seems some new feature is being added to get you to surf more and spend more time in that program.

Is there such a thing as too many features? The argument could be made that the more features you add, the less attention is being placed on the traffic. Surf bars have been replaced by arcade games in the case of Top Surfer, and while this is fine, how much attention is really being paid to the website below the surf bar?

On the other hand, it keeps people active. I have heard from numerous readers that say the only reason they click is for the maze to open up at Mystical Maze, or the new Clicks Matrix game or the poker game on Share Traffic. These people spend hours upon hours clicking and trying to win some extra hits, or maybe some cash even.

When it all comes down to it, I would say that the more UNIQUE features a hit exchange has, the better chance of having loyal members. People love to click, don't let the horror stories fool you, but they love to click when they are having fun. Features in a hit exchange make it FUN, and that is what creates happy members. When you have happy members, your traffic is always flowing.

Issue 53 – Whatever Happened To?

Some may remember the first few years that hit exchanges were online. Can you remember which programs were THE ones to surf? Do you remember which programs delivered the best results? I can, but it has changed a lot in only a few short years.

Hit Harvester, arguably one of the most popular hit exchanges ever, has almost slipped away completely. With porn site after porn site, virus after virus and frame breaker after frame breaker, it's amazing they still have people to click. Remember EZHits4U? Once one of the finest designed exchanges on the net, it is only on my mind because it's still in a few downline building sites that I'm a member of. Or how about the 'most popular start page on the net', No More Hits? Whatever happened to these heavyweights?

Simple, they forgot how to answer e-mails. Customer service seems to be a thing of the past for these programs, not only do they not seem to answer any e-mails, not a single 'update' e-mail has been sent in months. Or how about a re-design? To be a player in this industry, you need to keep things fresh. I think these program owners felt like they would always be on top of the game, so slowly their lead has diminished.

It really doesn't take much, only a few hours a day. Your members will appreciate an update every now and then. This does not mean send them some great 'discount sale package', but just to let them know you are still there for the program. It's really a shame because these programs have HUGE memberships, and hopefully, this article can stir up some emotion and put those programs back into action. Because to be honest, I miss those programs. They used to be the programs I would spend hours surfing on, and I look forward to a new look or new attitude from them soon.

From a member of over 3 years, please bring your programs back into the spotlight!

Issue 54 – Whatever Happened To Hard Work?

I'm absolutely amazed, each and every day when I fire up my computer and this is what I see;

Make money by doing nothing! Or *Join now for free, and retire in 3 months!*

Hmmm, did I miss something? Every day in Net Marketing Forum members are shown the latest, greatest 'hype du jour' in the Online Opportunity section. It's usually some program that promises riches and has a nifty photo of some middle-aged couple sailing away on a million dollar yacht. Hmmmm!

It doesn't happen like that, actually it's about 6 months of fighting with your spouse EXPLAINING to them that you are almost going to be able to pay the phone bill this month. Another 6 months of coming up with a winning concept and finally about a year to put it into motion....

OK, maybe not that long, but you know what it does take?

I feel like I'm swearing by saying this, but it takes... Work. Yes that dirty little four-letter word that seems to be posted everywhere online, but seldom is work actually accomplished. Yes, we all have lives and jobs outside of our little online business community and that's fine, but to think you can just sit back and watch the Pay Pal notifications roll in is plain silly.

Each and every day, hard-working business people make a living online. It's totally possible, I can name a dozen people in NMF right now who are making a good income online. But do I know billionaire gurus that sit back and watch the payments come in? Nope, and I don't want to know them either. I like being around hard-working people because it gives you energy. Being around positive people does that to you.

So if you are tired of all the hype and B.S. that happens online, I want you all to SWEAR right now with me... "I will WORK for a living!" OK, We all said we would, now let's all get to work! Keep on clicking and enjoy your WORK! =)

Issue 55 – The Perfect Clicker

Last week, I interviewed Tony Tezak, one of the most active and successful hit exchange users to ever pick up a mouse. That got me thinking, because of Tony's success at surfing the exchanges, what would be my idea of the perfect clicker? What kind of personality is required to do really well at hit exchange advertising? What does that person need to 'do' to become successful?

The perfect clicker must be dedicated. They must not get discouraged if they see their numbers drop, and they must not get too excited if they see their numbers soar. Slow and steady seems to be the best way to go. Have a goal and work towards it. If you want to hit 1,000 hits a day, work on a plan and stay focused until your reach that number.

The perfect clicker must NOT rely on their downline. Sure, it's great to get the residual traffic that hit exchanges provide, but they must not be afraid to get in front of their computer and click for an hour or so each day. Not only does this help the industry as a whole, it helps the clicker know what works for promoting different pages and what does not.

The perfect clicker must spend money. Yes, folks we are all trying to run some kind of business, and while the hit exchanges are free to use, buying traffic or upgrading in various hit exchanges is something everyone should look at. I mean, let's be real, your fingers do start to get tired after a session on TS 25 *lol*, so invest wisely in a hit exchange that gives you the best bang for your buck, and then get back to clicking the next day!

The perfect clicker must understand how hit exchanges work. The more they understand, the more they become effective promoters. They know that you won't be able to sign up any referrals on a copycat affiliate site that reads like an e-book, they know how to create smart and catchy doorway / splash pages.

And finally, the perfect clicker must have fun while surfing. Yes, it takes a lot of time and yes, it becomes 'boring', but they are excited because they know that with each and every click, that could mean a sale and / or a referral. If you do not have a love for what you are doing, you should not be doing it. This is why this could be the GREATEST industry to get involved in, because I don't know about you, but I love these programs!

Issue 57 – The Art of Support

I wanted to share a great e-mail I received this week. It's from a member of a hit exchange that was absolutely thrilled with the support they received when they e-mailed the owner. This is the e-mail I received, in it's complete form, not edited.

Hi Jon,

I had an interesting experience with Hit Safari recently and it highlighted quality customer service.

I had been surfing on Hit Safari but missed a few "Congratulations - you have won some bonus credits" pages. So my account was temporarily suspended and I was asked for an explanation.

I told the administrator in my response that when I see "congratulations" I tune out - you see so many "congratulations - you have won a free report...you are the 50,000 visitor...you have won an ebook, etc". In consequence, I missed clicking the verification page.

The administrator's response was:

"I've re-set your account. I appreciate your taking time to respond and I think you probably have a point. I'm also used to getting that as well, as the stop sign is on so many sites and is also used as a verification page. I'll change that in the next day or two at the most. Thanks again...

Paula support@hitsafari.com"

True to her word, Paula changed the "verification page" from "Congratulations" to the new little jumbo elephant (which you cannot miss!). And she did so within 12 hours!

Now that's service and respect for the views and experiences of the surfer!!

Cheers

Ron P.

Something to think about the next time you want to spend hours surfing a hit exchange, does the owner care about your opinions, and value your time online?

Issue 60 – The Art of The 'Doorway / Splash Page'

It should be mentioned that no matter how great a hit exchange is, it cannot be held accountable for lacklustre sales or referrals. Simply put, you've got to look at the website you are promoting and ask yourself, would this interest me if I was clicking for credits?

I can almost bet some of you are saying, "Absolutely not. I don't want to read an entire e-book when I'm clicking, I want to earn credits." Ah ha, Watson, a clue!

Folks, I know I sound like a broken record, but it is SO important that you create a basic doorway / splash page if you want to have real success in the hit exchanges. This is not to replace your affiliate URL, it's to add another dimension to your advertising arsenal. Simply put, people see the same sites day in and day out, you NEED to stick out like a sore thumb and the best campaigns ever to come into the industry have done just that.

So does that mean you need a flash presentation with booming music to grab someone's attention? While that may work for some, you do not need to go to that length. Just a QUICK loading website that is about a paragraph or two in length, outlining some key points about your program is good enough. Make sure if you need them to click on a link, it opens a new window. If you can, use some kind of email capture system and above all else, get a unique graphic and stick it right in front of everyone's eyes. Need help finding graphics? Go to Google and type in 'royalty free clipart', believe me, you'll find something.

What's the secret to successful hit exchange advertising? Is it splash / doorway pages? Maybe, but they certainly are a very good step in the right direction. Have fun with them, be creative and get the results you are looking for!

Issue 61 – Where Do We Go From Here?

So I got invited into Doug Williams (3 Step, Money Legs, Viral Visitors) new Best of the Best link directory. Or is it the Rest of The Best? I can't remember, that's not important. This idea on paper seems VERY solid. Get a bunch of hit exchange owners to link to each other's websites, and start to promote them offline. While Doug has some 'interesting' rules on how to be included in this directory, I applaud him for doing something many traffic exchange owners have not done!

Promote the industry offline! As you know, *MoneyLegs.com is home of the 200 Million offline classified ad campaign!* Good job! Finally, someone has stepped up to the plate and has come to the understanding that the future of hit exchange advertising is offline. We need new people to come into our industry, but will it take 200 million classified ads to do it? I don't know, but it's a start!

So why doesn't the entire industry follow suit? Hopefully, with the upcoming release of the Traffic Exchange Alliance, many of these promotion ideas can be put into motion, but I really think this is a good day for exchanges. Yeah, Doug does things his own way, and yeah, some people don't agree with his tactics, but let's all agree on something, the guy is a success!

So will I join the Rest of the Best? I'm not sure if I want to rent out prime time ad space for a Money Legs banner, but I guarantee you one thing, hit exchanges are about to get a lot more exposure in the upcoming months. If anything, it's got me thinking, and I hope offline advertising has got you excited too! Traffic exchanges are the perfect promotional tool, we just need more people to know about them!

Issue 62 – No More Than Four

I'm trying to really push this concept and make a lot of people stop and look at their surfing habits. I call it the **No More Than Four** campaign. I will be mentioning this in updates on my exchange, I Love Hits, as well as bringing it up in various forums across the Internet that deal with hit exchange promotion. Here's what I'm trying to get across...

As many of your know, multi tabbed browsers have become the 'norm' for surfing hit exchanges. Whether it be Firefox, Netscape, Myie2, Crazy Browser, Avant... They are everywhere. Most people that surf exchanges find them to be much easier to manage. Simply put, instead of opening up a new browser window for each program you are surfing, you open a new 'tab' within one single browser. As well, most of these programs have built in pop up killers, which makes surfing a breeze.

Because this is only one browser, it uses very low system resources on your computer. So basically, you can load up 20 or more different tabs (exchanges) and surf away. One problem, are you looking at any sites? Or just the timer to click 'next site'?

Folks, this whole 'campaign' of mine is not to tell you to sign up for every single program you view when you surf, because honestly, a lot of it is garbage. This is what I'm suggesting, open up no more than four tabs, and surf in groups. Read each website, and if you've seen it before, try scrolling down to see if there's anything that has been added. Basically, treat every single website you view when you surf like you want your own to be treated.

I know a lot of people will disagree and say, I'm not surfing to join a new program, I'm clicking for credits. That's fine, just show the website some respect, as well as your fellow surfer and just read or scan over the websites. If something peaks your interest, sign up, fill out a form, download an e-book. Remember, this entire industry is based on co-operation. We are exchanging traffic between ourselves, so let's remember how long it takes to earn those hits.

No More Than Four is not just a suggestion to only open 4 tabs at once, it's also a very effective way to manage your hit exchange advertising. Grouping your favorite hit exchanges into smaller groups lets you focus on each exchange and each site in rotation. Keeping this in mind, you may find much better success if we all treat each other's sites as we want ours to be treated.

It may not be the easy way to surf, but I bet it's a more effective way! =)

Issue 63 – Big Hmmmm's

A forum member in NMF (NetMarketingForum.com), Jon Atwood, recently reviewed some of the older posts in the forums. He went back a few months, and dug up some of the new 'guaranteed money makers', money doublers, and cash matrix programs. He discovered that the majority of them were either completely offline or were still in pre-launch. Yes, even after 6 months, some of these programs were still advertising their pre-launch date... 2 months ago!

What does this tell me? Simple, there is a LOT of garbage on the Internet and specifically in the hit exchanges. Folks, use some common sense when you are thinking of joining these kind of scams and schemes. Here's a few tips;

1. If it sounds too good to be true, it almost CERTAINLY is. Yup, that old saying is as true as ever. If they show some middle-aged couple laughing on their yachts, or testimonials THE DAY the program is released, and if they promise you some kind of income, run away.

2. Don't get caught in the hype. A solid business opportunity will be here and give you just as much chance to earn a buck in 2 months as it would in 2 days. Real businesses cannot just pop up and be an overnight success, chances are they will disappear just as quickly.

3. What's the track record of the program owner? Do you know the owner's name or their other businesses? If you KNOW that this owner has done some shady dealings in the past, why even take a risk?

Just a few tips. By no means is this a guide for anyone looking to start an online business, because there are hundreds of quality programs out there. It's just a concern of mine that so many people will put everything they have into something and then it will be gone in a month. Just like Mr. Atwood discovered in the NMF Opportunities Forum.

Do you remember the bubble games? Whatever happened to Spam Terminator? Or what about Cash Evolution? Remember Clickity Cash? Or even as recent as the randomizers? Don't get caught, protect yourself and investigate the claims, investigate the hype and if it sounds too good to be true....Hmmmm.......

Issue 64 – Reading Is Fundamental

If I am wrong here, please forgive me, but I think it's time this gets out in the open. Here's the question, is it me, or do people NOT read websites any more? I mean, when you join a new program, do you read the contents of the front page? Do you understand what you are joining? If you are spending money, is it clear on what you are receiving?

I had quite an interesting e-mail the other day from a new customer at Doctor Traffic. The first email was titled, "I hope this is legit!", the next was, "You misled me, this is supposed to be a banner exchange".... Please, if you are reading this, click on the link for Doctor Traffic, and tell me if ANYWHERE on the site that I mention it is a banner exchange. This person PAID me, and thought that he or she was joining a banner exchange? I don't even think I have the word banner in Doctor Traffic?

Folks, read before you click... Read before you join... And above all else, read before you pay someone. I mean, I saw that the person paid for something they did not want, so I refunded them immediately, but imagine all the scam artists out there that would take that money and run? I can almost understand now why all these 'get rich quick' schemes and 'guaranteed profits in a week' programs keep popping up, there are people that are not reading what they are getting themselves into.

Check out the sites, if they have testimonials, why not try to get a hold of the person giving the testimonial and get their feedback? Do a search in Google to see if the owner has had any 'problems online' in the past. Make sure you understand what you are getting yourself (and your business) into. I know hit exchanges have become more of a visual medium in recent months, and that's fine, but if a program has a lengthy ad copy...Read it all!

Issue 65 – Have I Found It?

There are some great downline builders (or clubs) online. Programs like MPAM, Rev 9, Traffic Hoopla, Traffic Tornado, Joe Shmo, and others each have their unique and impressive features. Some rely on the money making side of things, others remain focused on the hit exchanges they serve. I've always been a big fan of these programs, because MPAM is actually where I got my start in the industry many years ago (well, it seem like many years ago *lol*).

Profit Rally is different, though. I rarely promote programs I do not own in the hit exchanges, but this program is very special. If you have been surfing the exchanges lately, you must have noticed this site, I mean it's absolutely everywhere. And I'm going to tell you why it's number one in my books right now, and why thousands of people are joining this club.

Features! Profit Rally has got it all. This is THE complete advertising solution. Everything from ad trackers, to site rotators, to email capture, to auto responders, to downline mailers, even step by step training, this program has got it all. There is nothing this program does not cover. It's been bred for hit exchanges, and does an amazing job at not only building your downlines, but giving you some nice residual income as well.

The most important feature this program has is the different referral URLs you have used to promote your Profit Rally system. From general information pages to detailed descriptions of how their ad trackers work. And what else is so great, the owner is also a designer, so the layout is beautiful. *lol*. I get a warm fuzzy feeling when I log in and check out what it has to offer.

I know this sounds off the wall, but I really think this could be one of the most important websites for not only your hit exchange advertising, but also the industry as a whole. It has slowly built itself up, as there was little or no hype for it when Profit Rally launched.

Profit Rally continues to impress everyone that joins, and is a perfect example of what a downline builder can become. And you know what is the most exciting part of this? Axel (the owner) is newer to the hit exchange industry... Give him another 6 months and watch what he'll come up with!

Jon's Note: Profit Rally's owner has gone Missing In Action. We haven't heard from him in years. Checkout AffiliateFunnel.com for a much better downline builder. (end of shameless self promotion!)

Issue 66 – The Anti-Auto Man

Wow, have I ever caught some heat from disgruntled exchange owners and surfers over the past year and a half since I've been writing this e-zine. One of the biggest 'complaints' I get is my lack of support of the auto hit exchange industry. For those who have recently subscribed to Hit Exchange News, let it be known, Jon is NOT a fan of auto hit exchanges. An interesting discussion took place in a forum I frequent so I thought it would be a good idea to explain why I have never reviewed or featured auto hit exchanges.

It's not that I'm anti auto hit exchange, in fact, I think they are very remarkable systems. They have a very high user rate, most of the memberships are in the tens of thousands, and you can get a lot of traffic from using them. It's not even the quality of the traffic that makes me not use these programs. To tell you the truth, I'm basically anti auto anything.

I don't like automation online. I rarely use auto responders because I think it takes away from the 'human communication' we lack, especially online. For me, there is nothing better than reading a well thought out support request, not just an auto responded message. I was never a fan of FFA programs, and once the automation of the safe lists came about (and arguably ruined the industry), I ran away from that as well. I think there is WAY too much automation in the Internet marketing business, because it plays with the popular belief that it is easy to make money online. The whole 'sit back and let it happen' attitude if you will.

I'm living proof that YES there is money to be made online and NO, you don't need to be 'automated' to make it happen. I've actually had horrible experiences with automation, and way back when, accidently sent out over

100,000 emails via auto responder the first time I ever used an FFA program. I like being in control of my business and not relying on some piece of software to let my members know they are appreciated and valued.

I can admit it though, automation of online business is here and very popular. So no, I'm not anti auto hit exchange, I just like to know my sites are being viewed by real people. Think about it, we are all communicating everyday with people on the other side of the globe, all behind these boxes we call computers. I like to keep in mind that there are real people behind each of those computers...

Issue 68 – Where's The Exchange?

I've got to ask you something? If you had hundreds of credits stacked up in some account (the hit exchange will remain nameless) and even though you received about 2-3 hits PER DAY, you were told you have to surf a minimum of 50 sites per month to remain 'active'....Would you do it?

Here's my thing, if I receive 3 hits per day, and I'm surfing 30 per month PLUS I have thousands of hits already in my account, doesn't it make sense for that hit exchange to start delivering hits? Why should I continue to surf when the credits I have already earned are not being used?

Simple, a lot of hit exchanges have horrible credit inventory management and the excuse is for these people to continue to tell you that you have to remain in priority or active status to get your measly 3 hits per day.

How about this, these hit exchanges start delivering the credits and then I'll continue to surf. So the message here is, YES, you need to remain active in the exchanges, but if the program does not deliver... Where's the 'exchange' in hit exchange? You've done your part, when will the program do its part?

Still... We click on!

Issue 72 – 2004 In Review

What an impressive year it has been! 2004 has been a very good year for the hit exchange industry. A lot of new hit exchanges came online and some even went offline, which shows us that more people are understanding the responsibility that comes with owning a hit exchange. While this trend can alarm some, I think the focus for 2005 should be to bring more members into the exchanges. More members means more eyes looking at your website, this is a very good thing! Here's some of the top stories of the past year:

TS 25 was the largest hit exchange to launch this past year. The whole concept of rewarding people for being active was a great step forward. I applaud the folks at TS 25 for taking this approach, and hope that it rubs off with all new exchanges coming online.

The pro only hit exchange market has grown. While the jury is still out on the effectiveness of the programs, the important thing is that they are growing every day. I even got into the pro only swing of things and released Pro Traffic Shop. 2005 should prove if the pro only exchange will reach the expectations that a lot of us feel they will.

Clicksilo, one of the oldest hit exchanges on the net, went offline. No word, no notices, just a disappearing hit exchange. This was a loss to the industry as Click Silo was a very reliable and active hit exchange.

Profit Rally was launched to a lukewarm welcome, but as time grew, this program became one of, if not, the most effective downline builders online. What set this program apart was that once members joined the system, they actually signed up for the programs in it. A great design and very easy to use instructions made Profit Rally one of the must-have programs of 2004.

The Money Legs system made a HUGE push to start promoting their hit exchanges offline. This was a very welcomed approach to advertising our industry, and hopefully a lot of owners took notice. Offline promotion is such a great way to let the world know about the hit exchanges!

Many other stories were newsworthy, but all and all, 2004 was a great year to be involved in the hit exchanges. I think the big focus we as members of this industry should concentrate on for the new year is to get more people involved. We need to bring new people into the exchanges to not only make our advertising campaigns more effective, but also to brand the exchanges as a viable and effective form of advertising. What a great year it has been, and I wish you all nothing but success in the upcoming year. Keep on clicking!!!

Issue 74 – A Tip Or Two

To go along with the recent release of my new program <u>HitExchangeSurvivalKit.com</u>, I thought it would be good to go over what has worked for me in hit exchange advertising.

For as long as I can remember, hit exchanges have been a haven for affiliate programs and money making programs. To be put in a better way, everyone is promoting the same old sites, generic affiliate pages, etc.

The major problem I see with hit exchange users is that they don't realize the incredible opportunities that hit exchange traffic can generate. By promoting the same affiliate link as hundreds of others, you are in fact BRANDING that program owner's name. And that's fine. Here's a tip though, use those hundreds of other affiliate sites as branding for your custom splash page.

A splash page is a simple website that is created to promote another website.

All those hundreds of affiliate sites being promoted in the exchanges serves you if you promote a splash page of the program you are trying to advertise. People will be so used to seeing the same program over and over, but once they see your splash page advertising that affiliate program, it's almost a guarantee they will stop and look. Use the affiliates to your benefit and get your pages seen by everyone in the exchanges.

I've been 'preaching' the power of splash pages for years and they do work. Huge ad copy websites usually don't do well in the exchanges. Remember, quick loading, catchy headline, great graphic, key points and a request for more action (either a 'open a new window' link or an email capture form). Splash pages are the best kept secret online for success in the exchanges!

Issue 75 – The Power of Networking

Get involved! If there is anything that I can point to as a 'secret to success' online, it has to be the power of 'meeting other business people', A.K.A. Networking.

We are involved in the greatest business online. By using a computer, we can network with members from all sides of the planet. Our business is truly open 24 hours a day. We have just as much chance to make money at 3 am, as we do at 3 pm. There are so many ways to connect with other people online from forums, chat rooms, Instant Messengers, e-mail, blogs..... So why does it seem that less and less people are taking advantage of these great resources?

Let me 're-introduce' some folks to the wonderful world of NMF. Net Marketing Forum is a unique place, to say the least. The 'community' of exchange surfers, owners and business people alike have been online for quite some time now and is a GREAT place to network. It's free, it's fun and you get to meet a lot of great people. So how can you use this place to benefit your business?

Simple, get involved. Take part in the discussions, get some feedback from your homepage, join a program in the downline builder, meet hit exchange owners and get your questions answered. The single best thing this does, though, is get your name known. Branding is the key, folks, keeping your name in front of people's faces is very important online, and forums are a great place to do this.

How about meeting with people and communicating with them through voice chat? How about a stop by SWAT Traffic's conference room. A live voice over IP conference room that is full with program owners, surfers and again, people just like you! Have a burning question? This is the perfect place to ask it. Or if you just want to hang out and hear some of us 'yap' about hit exchanges, the chat room is the place to be.

The case in point, the resources are there and your most powerful tool is ready to be used. Do not underestimate the power of your NAME and your BRAND. This is what will make your mark online. Above all else, it puts back some personality in an industry where everyone seems to hide behind a computer screen name!!!

Issue 76 – The Dawn of the Alliances

I was in the Make 1 C conference room this week and I was asked a very interesting question. One of the members wanted to know why it seems some exchanges seem to group together. Some of the exchange owners in NMF seem to hang out with each other in chat rooms. Some other exchanges seem to group together in various Instant Messenger programs. Some consider themselves to be above everyone else and do not contact anyone. Why is that?

The alliances are brewing! A few months ago, a group of us that frequent NMF decided to create the Traffic Exchange Alliance. While this never did take off, the general idea is still in place and some program owners are still working on developing a strong foundation for this to proceed. Another group of people have recently started an association called the Traffic Exchange Owners Association, which has some smaller programs, but are way ahead of the rest of the alliances in development and implementation of a members page, forum and basic resources. Then there is a 'hush hush' association that has a group of smaller exchanges with an emphasis on building each program to be a stronger and more visible part of the industry.

The main point, and important issue I think is that it's progress. No matter which way you look at it, when people get together, good things happen. The real claim to fame will be if these associations can bring in the much-needed 'fresh set of eyes' by promoting hit exchanges on a much broader scale. That is when all this that we do, whether it's a newsletter, a hit exchange, a blog, or a forum post, really starts to pay off. I'm all for it.

Jon's Note: Whatever happened to this? If anyone is every interested in getting this thing started again, please get in touch with me!

Issue 77 – The Year of the Blog

What an incredible week it has been for me and my new program, Blogazoo.com. In 7 short days, Blog Azoo has grown from zero to 800 members, which I am delighted to say has been a huge wake up call for me.

Blog Explosion really did have something when they started the first blog-only hit exchange a few months ago. Jeff Trumble (of Webmaster Quest) approached me when it was about to launch and I was pretty reserved about it. I was not very blog savvy, ignorant to the entire community, and did not see the potential growth this could have.

A few months passed and then John Farrar of Wolf Surfer let me know he was having amazing results from his blog exchange called Blog Clicker. This got me thinking that blogs are something I, as a hit exchange enthusiast, should be looking into.

Folks, blogs are like going back in time to when content was king on the net. The amount of people that actually READ blogs and not just skim past them is remarkable. If you ever wanted to tell your side of the story or get your opinion heard (and we all know how much Jon loves opinions), blogs are for you.

Want even more proof that blogs are EXTREMELY popular and growing within the hit exchange industry, check out the newest addition to the Traffic Hoopla family of sites, Blog Hoopla.

These things are here to stay and I suggest to everyone, go get yourself a blog, start writing about what you believe in, or have an opinion about. Talk about your business experience, even talk about your hit exchange experiences. These are such a welcomed change from the same old 'matrix, forced, MLM' stuff we see every day online.

In my opinion, blogs bring back the sense of pride in one's website. It's free expression at its finest. And the best thing about blogging, there are no set boundaries. Talk about whatever you like and have fun with it!

Jon's Note: I currently do not own Blogazoo anymore, but I am in the 'blogosphere' with my HitExchangeBlog.com and AskJonOlson.com. Cool huh?

Issue 78 – Why Are There So Many Filters?

What is with all the spam filters? My goodness, how are you going to sign up for a program and then ask the owner to verify the email address? I really have a hard time trying to figure this one out.

What's funny to me is that most of the people who use these things still end up getting the 'body enhancement' e-mails, but won't get a H.E.N. or I Love Hits update. Then I get an e-mail about two months later that says, 'Why haven't I got your updates?'

Folks, use these filters with caution. You may never know what you are blocking when it's set on 'High'. I tried to use a spam filter about a year or so ago, and well, have you ever heard of Spam Terminator?

All joking aside, I understand the need for these filters, but if you are signing up for a program, there has to be some way to allow that program to get through your filters. There is nothing more annoying for a program owner than to get a 'confirmation e-mail' from some spam filter service.

Spam is bad, but not getting your H.E.N. is worse!

Issue 79 – The Death of the Exchanges?

Hit exchanges are not dying, don't worry. I just thought that would be a funny title to grab your attention. Any ways, another hit exchange is up for sale and the most recent is Racetraffic.com. While this may not be shocking news to some, it raises some very important questions.

First, I think a lot of us can agree that there are too many hit exchanges and not enough people surfing. While I applaud endeavors like the Free Advertising Giveaway and the various offline promotions that some exchanges are doing, there are still only a handful of people online that even know exchanges exist. Case in point, we need more surfers, that is a given.

That is a whole other topic, but the next thing that raises my eyebrows is people do not understand what it means to own and operate a hit exchange. First, it's not glorious. Ask any hit exchange owner, it could be WebmasterQuest or Click Crazey, these things take money, time and a lot of effort.

The problem is that people come online, see that they can run a business for peanuts and think the money comes rolling in. It doesn't, in fact, it takes years to develop these programs into true cash generators. And that is why hit exchanges seem to be going up for sale every week, it takes so much time and effort to get these things to run properly.

So this means, dare I say it, that not only do hit exchange owners need to work their tails off to generate traffic flow, they need to keep promoting to bring in new members. Hit exchanges aren't dying, they are just getting harder to operate and that is actually a good thing for the owner and the surfer alike.

I wonder where those 'alliances' have gone to? Seems to be a very good time to get them going again?

Issue 80 – The Auto Surf Debate Part 23432

Ho hum, looks like Jon struck a nerve again with some auto hit exchange faithful. This past week, I got into quite a heated e-mail debate with the owner of an auto hit exchange about the validity of the auto exchange concept. While it's no secret how I feel about these programs, it's something that still seems to strike a nerve with some folks.

I gave up trying to 'change people's opinion' about auto hit exchanges, because we are all grown adults and make decisions for ourselves. So my argument with the owner was not based on their program, but rather my opinion on the popular auto hit exchange mentality.

Does this sound familiar? *"I'm too tired to click, my hand hurts when I surf, it's so boring to click in a manual exchange, auto hit programs are easy because I can set them up, not look at any sites, go to bed and then when I wake up, have a hit counter spinning."*

That is what I consider the auto hit exchange mentality. I am NOT anti auto hit exchange, but rather against the promotion of lazy people. This falls in line with this myth that exists online about 'Pay me 20 bucks and you'll be rich in 20 days'. There is no quick way to making real income online, and there is no quick way to build a successful traffic campaign. It all takes work, effort and a lot of elbow grease.

Issue 81 – Please Check Your Rotators

Want to know how to make every hit exchange owner on the Internet really upset? Stick a frame breaker in your ad tracker and then throw it into a rotator!

It's time someone said it, please, check ALL your URLs that you want to add to your rotator. I know it's a great tool, and you can add hundreds of sites to it, but when your site pops up in a hit exchange and gets reported for frame breaking, chances are the owner will suspend your account or even remove it if it's a rotator.

Some owners have stated that it's not their job to police a rotator, and I agree. I have even been known to have had a bad URL slip through my watchful eye as well, so it is so important to manage your rotators. Check each URL thoroughly, if you feel like it may be a frame breaker, or some kind of malicious download site, get rid of it.

Remember, not only does this annoy the hit exchange owner, but your fellow surfers are suffering as well. This just goes back to the concept of 'treat others like you want to be treated', manage your rotator!

Please, it makes surfing so much more enjoyable!

Issue 84 – Exchange Specific Advertising (E.S.A.)

Have you ever been surfing MPAM Start and thought, W*ow, there are a lot of MPAM pages in rotation.* Or what about 10Khits4unow, Viral Visitors or Clickaholics? Did you notice more and more Money Legs sites?

Here's something to ponder when you are about to create a new website for your hit exchange advertising. Most of the 'hubs' or businesses that frequent the exchanges also have their own programs, so why not create exchange specific ads for the program you are promoting?

For example, instead of saying on your website, *"Stop clicking and check this out"*, why not add a little plug for the exchange you are promoting in. An example would be, *"Hey MPAM Start members, check this out!"*

It does not even have to stop there. Think of all the people promoting the latest and greatest 'scam'... I mean, online money maker in the exchanges. Target them! Get their attention and play on their experiences. I remember a few years ago, there was a very popular program that everyone seemed to be a member of. However, the website seemed to be offline more than it was online. One of my greatest exchange promotions back then really focused on all the downtime those people were experiencing. Relate to your viewer, you will see much better results!

Issue 85 – The Game Plan

Game plans are very important when you want to start a business. The truth be told, when I got started, I had no idea what I was doing. I clicked for an hour at Hit Harvester and then took 4 days off while I was working offline. And then jumped back on, spent about 40 dollars on some 'anti spam money maker' that went belly up and then took another 3 days off to flip pizzas...

Chances are, if you are just getting started in this business, you are not working this on a full-time basis. Some of you, perhaps, are, but for the majority of the surfers online, this is just a part-time gig. Trust me, organize yourself now. Even if you are new to this and plan on taking it very slow, it is so much easier to set up a 'planned week' for your surfing.

There are so many great downline builders that can help you manage your business with set schedules, training, live seminars and all the tools you'll need to get off on the right foot. And hey, even if you are an experienced hit exchange surfer, it would not hurt to know which exchanges you want to surf on the weekends.

There's this old saying, *'If you fail to plan, you plan to fail',* and it's so true in business. Set up a daily schedule for checking your emails, a time for taking a break, time for surfing and of course, time for picking up the kids from school. Remember, this is a business and if you treat it as such, you will be pleasantly surprised at the results.

Issue 86 – Jon The Auto Surfer

For as long as I can remember, I could not use auto hit exchanges. Maybe it was the fact that I tried them once and never got any results? Maybe it was because I thought they only attracted lazy surfers and people trying to make a quick buck, and not sustain a real business?

I asked a question in a poll about a month or so ago about how many people use these programs, and there are a lot of HEN readers that use them. It made me think if I should re-visit and test them again? I had written them off and while I did perform a 'test' on them a few years ago, I felt like it was time for me to give it another shot.

So with my trusty splash page, off I went to the 'big boy' of auto hit exchanges, Studio Traffic. Here's my 'journal' of what I have experienced so far.

First, it took 4 days and two emails to get my little splash page approved from them. According to their TOS, if you submit a URL and it does not get any response or approval, it's because you are breaking their terms. Everything looked fine, so I submitted it again. Day 4, my URL was approved.

So I started 'surfing' and wow, imagine my surprise when I checked my account an hour later. I was 1998 hits in the negative? By surfing about 50-70 sites, I had lost over 2000 credits and now sat in the hole. I tried to surf again yesterday, and while my 'account hits' were apparently going up, my hit counter on my splash page remained the same.

I shut everything down and just before I started writing HEN late last night, I could not even log into my account any more? So will I write off auto hit exchanges again? Not yet, this must be a very bad experience, so like I said in NMF this week, I'll give it a few more days and test out some other auto surf exchanges armed with my trusty splash page and hit counters. Stay tuned for the adventures of Jon The Auto Surfer, Part 2

Issue 88 – The 'Secret'

Have you ever wondered why brand names like Coca Cola, Wal Mart, Pepsi, or Target have such huge success? Well, of course they are multi-national corporations with millions upon millions of dollars in advertising budgets, but let's look at something very closely...

They understand how to advertise. Plain and simple, they have created their business because they know that advertising works, and getting their brand name in front of your eyes is the single most important thing they can do. Not only to grow their business, but also to maintain it.

How is this any different from hit exchange advertising? It's not.

What programs are the most successful online? The ones that are promoted the most? Maybe. The ones that generate the most money? Could be. Personally, I think it's because the owners of the business understand the importance of getting their message across to as many people as possible, and as often as possible.

What about that old tale that says you have to have 100% unique percentage in a hit exchange? Hogwash. In fact, I would prefer to have my sites seen quite a few times over, because it shows those few people surfing that I am advertising MY business and you are going to hear my message and see it.

Give it a try. Take whatever business you are promoting, and focus on it. Promote it as heavily as possible for the next week or so, and check your results. Don't promote 15 different pages, don't promote 10 different money makers. Pick one and concentrate all your efforts on it.

I myself am trying to adopt the concept of branding for my businesses STRICTLY in the hit exchange arena, and it's become a very powerful tool. Focus on one thing, work your tail off to brand it to you and do not slow down. You may be very surprised at the results.

Issue 90 – 7 Steps To TE Success

Tip 1 - Find yourself a 'starting point'! You will need a place to build your network of hit exchanges, and a secure program that grows with the industry. That is why I highly suggest joining AffiliateFunnel.com. This is a 'business center' that has everything you will need to use in your hit exchange advertising arsenal. It is what we like to call a 'downline builder', and not only will you find the best hit exchanges on the net in this easy to use system, you can also discover the many useful and effective tools for your hit exchange campaigns. This site has it all, and again, with its easy to follow instructions, your Profit Rally system can be up and running in no time.

Tip 2 - Become comfortable with all the tools and terms within the hit exchange industry. Learn what is a surf ratio, what a downline is, where a surf bar is located, and the dozens of other hit exchange terms that are around. **Take your time!** There is absolutely no rush in this business, you have to take your time and make sure you understand everything.

Tip 3 - Network! Join NetMarketingForum.com and introduce yourself to the world. Actually, join as many online forums as possible, especially if you are trying to build a business, and get to know your fellow entrepreneurs. Introduce yourself in the forums and spend a few hours poking around different topics of discussion. Not only is this a great learning experience, but you never know who you will meet in a forum. Many of the people I first met in the online forums are now my business partners and associates. This is the MOST VALUABLE resource you have online, use it and meet the world!

Tip 4 - Keep focused. It's very easy to get lost in the shuffle and even easier to get swept away by all the big hype and big nonsense that frequents the hit exchange arena. Remember this if nothing else: *if it sounds too good to be true, it probably is*. If some website is promising millions, it's best that you run for cover. However, this is where your 'network from Lesson 3' will come into play. If you have a question, ask around and see what other people's experiences may have been with it. So, the key to this is very simple, once you have found your program or business of choice, buckle down and remain focused. Speaking of which....

Tip 5 - What is your business? Be a leader, not a follower! If you have a good idea, put it on paper. If you think that new website you just created may be popular, start to promote it. If you are already a member of a program, keep at it! Find what you are good at, and work with that. I started writing about hit exchanges because I was good at working with them. It's a natural progression and if you search for it, you will find your reason for being online as well! We can all make a living online, it just takes time and effort, and a whole lot of networking.

Tip 6 - Do not be afraid to ask questions! There is no such thing as a bad question, and for my years of working online, I have heard this all too many times, 'I don't want to sound dumb'. Everyone was new to this industry once, so do not hide any questions which you may have. Ask in the forums, e-mail me, phone me, write me a letter, just get the question answered. You will feel a lot better about your time online when you have an understanding of what you are working with. Hit exchanges can be quite complicated at times, there is absolutely nothing wrong with asking that burning question!

Tip 7 - Have fun! It's that simple. Work hard at your business, put in the time and effort you would in any business, and use the tools that are around you. However, if you are not enjoying yourself, what is the point? I love my job, I love working from home and I would not trade it for the world. I used to flip pizzas about 4 years ago, and while I made money, it was not making me happy. You should ENJOY your time online and your brand new business! It's yours!

Issue 91 – The Anatomy of a Killer Splash Page

The creative side of hit exchange promotions is a tricky subject. For example, while you always want to try new and different ways to design a splash page, tried and tested practices do seem to do the trick.

Yes, the 'stop sign' graphic still works and yes, the headline, 'Are you tired of clicking' still gets the occasional glance. In this week's 'Deep Thoughts', let's really break down what has worked in successful splash page design.

Rule number 1, you need an eye popping graphic and headline! That is why the stop sign is so popular, because it really grabs your attention. That is exactly what you want to do when designing a splash page. Remember, 2-3 seconds is all you have to make a lasting impression on your viewer. Your graphic and headline are critical. This should be the two things about your splash page you work on the most. Find yourself a GREAT graphic and always change the headline until you find one that really works well in combination with your graphic.

The next tip would be to keep it simple. There is absolutely no point in writing a short novel on your splash page. A few sentences, or maybe one small paragraph to peak your viewer's interest is all you need. Remember, don't try to sell your viewer on the splash page, that is what the ad copy on your main site is for. Your viewers will be less interested in something that takes 45 seconds to read instead of creating curiosity with a few quick points, questions or sentences. Remember, keep it simple.

And finally, always request an action. Whether it be a bookmark, a 'click here to open a new window', or an e-mail capture form, make sure your viewer DOES something instead of just leaving the splash page. What good is the best graphic and headline in the world, if people who WANT more information cannot access it?

Splash pages are one of the most effective tools you can use for any hit exchange advertising campaign. I always use this analogy in all my seminars, think of a splash page like a billboard you see on the side of the road while driving. The advertisers know you will not pull your car over and run to the store to buy their product, however, if you see that billboard enough, chances are when you are in the stores you will remember their product. Get their attention and keep your pages in front of the viewer as much as possible!

Issue 92 – The Splash Banner

Sometimes I surf these hit exchanges so much. Click this color, click that color. Match this image, don't click this link. Sure, surfing for credits is not the most 'exciting' thing to do, but I try to enjoy myself. I always check out the pages, and maybe get some ideas for a new web page design. If I see something that peaks my interest, I'll sign up or purchase it.

Where are most people's eyes when they are surfing the exchanges? Yes, in a perfect world they would be focused right on your website, eagerly awaiting to see your PayPal button to purchase your product. Let's be honest, most people are looking at the timers or the surf bars.

Perfect!

I came up with this idea, because splash pages are the best way to use the hit exchanges, but still, most people's eyes are focused elsewhere. I call them *splash banners* for a lack of a better term, and they work!

I had some amazing click through rates this past week with some banners I created, and even got some paying customers. All from a simple, quick loading, eye catching 'banner'. No images, no fancy graphics, just the exact same concept of a splash page, but in banner format. Combined with a powerful splash page, these banners are a great companion to your hit exchange campaigns!

I am now developing these banners and started a new 'program' called SplashBanners.com. I will be working on putting together the new site, but wanted to let everyone know about them this week. Check out SplashBanners.com for more information on my new little idea.

Issue 93 – L.C.S.S.

I'm absolutely beside myself at some of the responses I've been getting recently or lack thereof when I have a support request at some exchanges. So here is my rant of the week...

I will stop surfing the exchanges that refuse to answer emails!

Hey, I understand that this may not be a full-time job for some hit exchange owners, that's fine. However, there is no reason to completely ignore e-mails or copy and paste some lame duck answer to commonly asked questions.

If you have ever suffered from the 'LCSS' *(Lack of Customer Service Syndrome),* the biggest message you can send these owners is this... Stop surfing their exchange. If you have issues that have never been addressed, or made a purchase and never had the credits added to your account, or just plain sick of the copy and paste support answers, hit them where it hurts, their user activity.

Stop surfing these programs that come up with excuse after excuse about *how they can't deliver traffic because,* or they *did not respond to your request because you did not do this.* It's time for the surfers to support the exchanges that care about their members. It's time to become active in the programs that you see trying to make this a better industry!

We each have something so important that every owner wants us to give them... Our time. Our time surfing their exchange, our time promoting their exchange... Now how about they give us 30 seconds of their time to respond to our e-mails? Hmmmm.....

Issue 95 – The Active Exchange Owner

What do you like most about your favorite hit exchange? Is it the games you play while surfing? The design? How about the quality of traffic? Yes, I am an owner, but before I ever owned any hit exchange, I was (and still am) an avid hit exchange surfer.

That being said, I'm going to outline what I think is the 'perfect hit exchange owner'. Yeah, it would be easy for me to say that I'm a wonderful exchange owner, but I'm still learning just as much as the next person. I am not happy with my hit exchange, and probably won't be until I have half a million members. So what are some great traits for a great owner?

They must be in tune with their program. These exchange owners do their best to make changes in the best interest of the program. For example, a few months ago, Hit Hurricane was going nowhere fast. I applaud the original owner, Mike Molloy, for handing the reigns over to a new owner when it was clear the exchange needed a change. And I applaud Jon Atwood for turning Hit Hurricane around into a very good program.

I also applaud the owners that listen to what their members want. Some people wanted more splash pages, the folks at Deep Sea Hits delivered. People wanted more games, WebmasterQuest developed a new poker game. This is what makes a hit exchange stand above the rest, pro active ownership.

Love him or hate him, I applaud Doug Williams for taking the hit exchange concept and advertising it to an offline market. Pro active ownership.

Some folks tell me that this industry is flooded with new hit exchanges. I say, let's flood the industry with pro active owners. People that aren't afraid to spend the thousands of dollars and the years of effort to make their hit exchange a great place to surf. As a surfer, to each and every owner that has ever taken that extra step, thank you!

So this is the real question...What has your favorite traffic exchange done for you lately?

Jon's Note: Doug Williams passed away in 2006. Doug was one of the first people I interviewed in Hit Exchange News and to this day is one of the greatest traffic exchange owners ever. The industry owes a lot to this man and I thank him for his vision and hard work. We lost a great leader.

Issue 96 – Your Investment

Everybody comes online looking to 'make money and start to work full-time from home'. This is the dream of so many people in this business and rightfully so, I mean the greatest feeling in the world is getting up and developing your business and your brand. I can think of nothing more rewarding than owning your own business, it really is a wonderful thing.

How long does it take? What is that magic number? Days, weeks, months, or is it years? I'll give you my opinion on it, it's the latter. Yes, forget all those 'get rich quick' schemes you have read about. All those doublers and randomizers that promised you that you could sit back and let the money come rolling in. They do not exist. Here's the truth, it takes an investment of a few years to get these things going.

Let me say it again, you will NOT get rich from surfing a hit exchange and you probably won't be making a decent income off them for at least 6 months. Why? Simple, you should be trying to, and are in the process of building a 'business'.

Go offline, try to start a business and the turnaround 'number' seems to be between 3 to 5 years, before a new business takes shape and starts earning the owner a profit. Yes, the Internet can cut this down, but not in the amount of time most 'hype machine' programs promise.

That being said, you have to develop your business and your name online. If you have been surfing a hit exchange for a month and see no results, try a new splash page, switch up your surfing schedule, but never give up. That's the easy road and the way to pin blame on someone or something else. The fact is, this business needs to be constantly attended to and grown into something solid.

Yeah, I'll say it. You need to keep surfing! You need to keep that upgraded membership. You need to pay your membership dues! You need to invest your time! You need to invest money! You need to stay in front of people's faces! You need to stay focused!

This is what has worked for me, nothing more and nothing less. I have only been working 'full-time' online for about 12 months in my 6-year career. So for those first 4-5 years I worked my tail off, and did the grunt work. It was not easy and it took a lot of time, but you know what, looking back it was worth the investment. The investment in myself and my dreams. Keep going, and don't stop promoting yourself!

Issue 97 – Don't Believe The Hype

Oh wow, this is always a fun topic. Ready? Here it goes!

When you use a traffic exchange, high unique hit percentages means squat!

That's right. All those programs that brag and boast about high unique hit percentages, and the people telling you that you need to have 100% unique traffic when using the exchanges do not understand one fundamental thing about advertising... How to build your brand!

Think of it like Coke and Pepsi (a popular analogy I use from time to time). Do you think that Coke and Pepsi spend millions upon millions to find new customers? Nope, they have as many customers as they will ever need and quite possibly most of the world's population knows what a Coke bottle is. Do you think someone that has spent only a few years online knows more about branding and advertising than arguably the biggest branding successes in known history? Nope. These BILLION dollar companies know that to stay on top, you need to stay in people's faces. Out of sight, out of mind does not work in the advertising world.

This means keeping your site in front of people over and over again. Now let me say this, a hit exchange giving you 1% unique hit percentages is obviously not the best investment on your time, and a good number to play with is between 30-70% unique. However, what if that one person that saw your site 10 times in one session starts to recognize you and your web site?

The popular saying in advertising is that it takes a potential customer between 7 to 10 times before they 'consider a purchase'. So what good is 100% unique traffic? That means you have had 100 people see your site and never come back. And as you well know in traffic exchanges, you don't get a lot of time to make an impression.

Yes folks, I will catch a lot of heat from this, but I do stand by it. Why? It works for Coke and Pepsi and it has been working for me. I have had the most success in this business when my name, logos and web sites are in front of people as much as possible. Try it and try to worry less about unique hit percentages, and focus more on the concept of advertising and branding your name. You may be pleasantly surprised!

Issue 98 – OMG It's A 404 Page!

Here's something I never understood. Why on earth do traffic exchange owners 'suspend' your URL if it does not load? How does this hurt their exchange? How does it inconvenience the surfer? You mean to tell me that the surfer would rather see 'Make Money Ripping Off People With This Brand New MLM Forced Matrix Mumbo Jumbo' than a 404 error page that will most likely be back online in 4 minutes?

It blows my mind. I mean, every site on the net does not have 100% up-time, things go offline, there are servers being moved, DNS issues, and a host of other situations that can cause a site to show an error for a few minutes. Let it slide!

Hey, it's not hurting anyone but the person promoting that site, it's not a frame breaker, there is no virus on the site. It just did not load properly. But each and every day, like clockwork, I need to log into some traffic exchanges and 're-submit' my URL for approval because it got reported for being 'offline'. I've even had some support e-mails telling me they are tired of it getting reported and were furious that I allowed my site to go 'offline for 5 minutes'!!!

I guess I think the effort could be placed in a more productive direction, like for example, frame breakers? Viruses? Things that really 'effect' the way we surf the exchanges.

Issue 99 – The Summer Slow Down Myth

I don't know where this urban legend came from, and I laugh each and every time I hear it. Maybe I run my businesses different? Maybe I have a very odd business practice? Or maybe it's just an excuse?

The popular notion that the summer months seem to grind this industry to a halt is the biggest bunch of bull I've ever heard (for lack of a better term). Last year, at this time, my co-op DoctorTraffic.net experienced the biggest jump in customers for the entire year of 2004. This summer, even though I have been away for the past 2 weeks, has once again been some of the best months of the year to date. Are my businesses abnormal or something?

Let's put it into perspective, from the 'real world'. When it's the summer, do the stock exchanges stop opening and closing? With the exception of students and teachers, do people get to sleep in during the summer months and not go to work? Did you tell your boss last week that it's hot outside so you won't be in to the office? See what I'm getting at? The world does not stop for summer and neither should we. Are less people surfing the exchanges? Not on my watch they are not, but even if they are, great! That means the people you want seeing your site are the ones surfing the most, the people that treat this like a business and not like a summer holiday.

I apologize for the rant this week, but I think this myth is getting old. This is prime time for your business. This is prime time to be surfing the exchanges. Are you in North America? Guess what, half of the planet (and arguably some of the biggest untapped markets online) are in the middle of winter these next few months, so start promoting your stuff! Get out there and get your web site seen by the people you really want to get it in front of, the people that are working their tails off!

An excuse? Maybe, but I look at it like a big opportunity. Let everyone else say there's a slow down, when you are speeding up!

Issue 100 – The Past 24 Months

Be warned, this is a 'big' article. It would take me a few hours I think to go over some of the most newsworthy items to take place in the first two years of H.E.N.'s existence, but I thought I would go over a few of them in this week's issue.

Like it or not, TS 25 is quite possibly the biggest news story of the past 2 years. Why? Simple, Logiscape changed the way we surf and think about a traffic exchange. They threw the whole concept of '1:1 surf ratios are the best' out the door (their 5:1 and 5:2 ratios showed people how to get traffic without the need for a 1:1 ratio). Their method of referral building completely shook up the industry, gone was the idea that the more you refer, the more you get. They showed members that in order to get traffic, you have to surf your butt off. It works as TS and Traffic Pods are some of the most active exchanges online. When all is said and done, the Logiscape people have made their mark!

The end of the MPAM-era in traffic downline building and the emergence of power builders like Profit Rally, Joe Shmo 200 and Traffic Tornado. For years, MPAM was *the* downline builder for tens of thousands of exchange surfers. In the past 6 months or so, MPAM has focused more towards search engine placement, and slowly veered away from the exchanges, while still being one of the best educational courses online, MPAM has now become much more than just a 'downline builder'.

The 'Pro Only Exchange' debate! Are they really a force in the business, or just an overnight fad? Well, if Click Master Pro and 123 Clicks are any indication, pro only exchanges are here for the long run. Have they become the be all and end all of exchange advertising? Not by a long shot, but nothing seems to get the blood boiling more than a new pro only exchange being launched. I think of them as another option, not a better option, not a worse option, just a different option. So much so, that I partnered with Dan Moses and created Pro Traffic Shop.

Auto surf exchanges.... While some manual traffic exchanges struggle to generate 1000 members, the auto surf programs could generate tens of thousands of members in a few short months. With the addition of the 'paid to auto surf function' some people have turned this once 'offshoot' of the manual exchanges into a niche all by itself. Yes, the jury, in my opinion is still out on how effective they are! What do you think?

The 'Blog Exchange'! As many have said, 2005 is the year of the blog and if Blog Explosion, Blog Soldiers, Blog Azoo and Blog Clicker are any indication, 2006 will be an even bigger year for blog traffic generating. Blog exchanges have become quite the useful tool for bloggers to get traffic to their site, more importantly, it has introduced a BIG market to the world of exchange traffic generation.

The 'Splash Page', and the effectiveness of good traffic exchange advertising. More and more people are coming to realize that to do well in this business, you need to get your message out there quickly, and as much as possible. Splash pages have allowed everyday surfers to create a name for themselves that was once unheard of in the copy-cat affiliate site. Are you promoting a business? No problem, get a splash page, stick your picture on it and brand not only that business, but your name as well. Effective exchange advertising is still the most important lesson people need to learn on these programs!

Trust me, there are hundreds of other news stories that made us all stop and do a double take, so for this second anniversary issue, let's see what you think! What do you think was the biggest news story in the traffic exchange industry in the past 2 years? Was it the Logiscape releases of TS25 and Traffic Pods? How about the emergence of the splash page? The pro only exchange debate? The blog exchanges? How about the influx of 10$ exchange scripts? Auto surfs? The PTP invasion?

Issue 103 – Think For Yourself

With the recent change of policy concerning downline credits and referral bonuses from programs like Click Crazey and Advertising Know How, it's amazing to see 'big changes' like this in the industry. Let's be honest, and I know this will upset many, but the exchange industry is a business that follows.

One exchange owners does something, the chances are someone else will follow their lead. A bunch of people start saying 'XYZ Matrix' will be the next big thing, it's promoted everywhere. It's not just in the exchanges either, it's online business in general. I had a chance to read an article by a very popular 'online guru' and he basically said it like this, most people in this business follow the leader. It's the pack mentality we as humans have had instilled in us since the creation of time. It's not a bad thing, it's just who we are. So when AKH and Click Crazey do things like 'take away' referral bonuses and the ability to earn credits from your downline's effort, it really makes you stand up and take notice.

Is it a good idea to take away referral bonuses? Not sure. I don't claim to know the answer because it's only been about a week since the changes have been in place, but bravo to the owners for doing something different. Now the big question is, who will be next?

If this trend does take off, it's almost a guarantee other owners will follow suit. Remember the popular 'Green Zap' program, which was being hailed as the next best thing online (a replacement to PayPal), well not only did everyone and their mother promote this thing a few months back, but it's yet to materialize. People are comfortable being 'normal' and following the pack. So if the majority promote it, there's a good chance even more will follow suit.

It's time for exchange owners to try something different. Stand out there and make your voice heard. Do something that may not make everyone smile, but will make people look. Go against the grain. Most of the biggest successes in human history happen when people step outside their comfort zone and do things differently. Like the popular slogan goes, *different is good!*

Issue 104 – The Design Dilemma

Is there no creativity left in our industry?

Take for example, the ever popular 'Stop Sign' graphic found on splash pages across the Internet. Why does every new splash page out there have a stop sign graphic? I think there are other 'traffic signs' we can use, but still we stick with the good old-fashioned red and white? That is minor compared to some of the other goodies I have noticed.

I love this one, how about the 'stock pictures' of some young professional guy and girl, huddled over the computer trying to look like they are so focused on business and nothing else? You know, the graphics that seem to come with the cookie cutter business scripts some people promoted during the past few months? The ones that are trying to add 'instant credibility' to a doubling program with the 'college students graphic'?

Those are just two examples in the problem I am seeing with web design in this business. There is no creativity left. If it's not being copied, it's just being recycled! Heaven forbid you actually hire someone to make you a custom graphic or logo. Folks, if you are looking to get the most bang from your traffic exchange experience, let me put it this way, your design and logos are HUGE factors. People can smell stock photos and trust me, these do not pull in sales and leads.

Hire a designer. Do a search in Google for 'cheap logos'. Find unique pictures. Dig deep for your design needs and you will find a wealth of great graphics. They are out there! If you need help finding any logos or graphics, drop me a line and I'll point you in the right direction!

Remember, in this business, sticking out from the crowd is what works!

Issue 105 – Run, Don't Walk

Here's a tip that I'm sure to catch a LOT of heat for, but it has to be said...

If a traffic exchange tells you they do not allow a link tracker (ad tracker), run away, don't walk, run! Stay as far away from any program that tells you they do not allow you to track your own stats. What are they hiding? Why won't they allow you to find out for yourself, by being a responsible business owner, what exchange is delivering and which ones are not?

More and more it seems traffic exchanges are not only telling you what you can and cannot promote in their programs, but some are even going as far to say you cannot use your own link trackers. Are you kidding me? Folks, other than splash pages, I'm not sure there can be a more important tool that you MUST be using. However, these owners are very quick to tell you , 'no trackers or redirects allowed'!!!

Their argument would be 'they break frames, there are viruses, the sites are illegal'... Baloney! I run one of the largeest traffic exchanges on the planet, and guess how many 'ad trackers' get reported in a day? Zero. The folks that use ad trackers are usually the people dead serious about their business and would never risk their account by inserting abusive sites in their trackers. So an owner telling you they have to search for hours to find abusive sites in an ad tracker is hiding something, because it takes all of 3 seconds to remove abusive sites from an exchange.

Why would owners be trying to prevent you for finding out for yourself exactly how that program is performing? So if an owner starts to tell you that you cannot use your ad trackers, find an exchange that allows them. Better yet, find an exchange that *suggests* that you use them. You have the power to find out exactly what works and what does not in this business, through ad tracking. And you have the power to send a message to owners preventing you to do so.

Say YES to ad tracking!

Issue 106 – The Rome Factor

Bigger! Better! Faster! I want it now! I want millions!

That seems to be the popular thought process of the majority of people that join this business. I do not know who to point the finger at, maybe even myself because I have fallen victim to the lies and hype so many times before, but why must we keep feeding these beasts?

Let's put it this way, success is NOT achieved in this business by jumping ship every 2 weeks. I call it slot machine marketing, and the 'gurus' call it their meal ticket. Folks, it takes time to build a business. Whether it's online, offline or elsewhere, real results are not measured by how quick you get in on a new matrix. It's not determined by how many people you refer to a program in a week. It takes time and effort!

I get e-mails every week from people that are fed up with a business after only a month or two of promoting it! Let's be honest, what REAL business can you name that has put the owners into profit after only 2 months of work? What about the months of planning before the program was launched? What about the endless hours of programming? Marketing? Analysis? Not to mention the money! It does not happen overnight.

I urge you to rethink joining that brand new matrix that got released last week. Or that wonderful auto surf that promises millions from simply 're-investing'... Take your time! Build the groundwork for a successful business model. If you are involved in an affiliate program, get involved in it and see what you can do to help out. Just don't jump ship when things get rough.

I hate using 'popular sayings', but this one is so true... *Rome was not built in a day!* And your online business shouldn't be either.

Issue 107 – Where To Surf?

One of the more popular questions I get asked every week is how can I tell which exchange is worth surfing and which ones should I buy credits from? The easy answer (which I have given many times) is to go with the exchange that feel the best to you. The one with responsive administrators and above all else, delivers what is promised. However, let's take a closer look at what makes an excellent traffic exchange.

Persistent advertising is a term that gets thrown around from time to time in this business, and it holds truth to which exchanges you should focus your energies on. Very simply put, the more you see an exchange and for the longer amount of time, chances are this owner is not only growing their business, but people are getting results from it.

Ask yourself this, would someone who owns an exchange that they think of as a hobby spend hundreds of dollars a week in advertising their program? Would a fly-by-night operation spend thousands on site development, updates and new features? Would a 'here now, gone tomorrow' traffic exchange be seen in other programs week after week after week? Chances are no, they would not. So there is your answer.

It's time to focus our time and effort with the exchanges that are doing their part. If you see Traffic Pods being advertised every day, chances are that exchange is delivering what is promised. If you are sick of seeing Hit Safari splash pages, guess what, someone is working their tail off to make that exchange great. *Jim Bob's A Plus Traffic Exchange* may not be the best bet for your time and effort, you have to go with what works!

You want results, you deserve them too. Go with the programs that are showing you, they are here to stay!

Issue 108 – I'm A Convert

I can admit it! I used to be the biggest fan and user of Crazy Browser (or whatever it's called these days). It was THE only browser I surfed with. When people would say they used a different browser I would be in shock. Crazy Browser was one of THE original multi-tabbed browsers that seemed to be tailor made for us exchange users. Even though they still say they have no idea what a traffic exchange is. Hmmm.

Anyways, while using Crazy Browser I was introduced to my good friend *virus*, his brother *key logger* and their cousin *trojan*. Let's put it this way, I just spent the last few weeks arguing with a tech guy about how much I should pay him to get the bugs off my computer. Folks, the 'Virus Boys' are no fun!

So a few months ago, I made the switch. I started to hear those two words in my ear every day from fellow surfers and I am now a convert. I have embraced Fire Fox. I mean, I don't think a multi-tabbed browser gets any better than this. Are you tired of flash presentations? Don't download the plug in. Sick of audio on web sites? Don't install the plug in. Not sure if you want trojan, key logger and virus to stop by for dinner? Use Firefox!

This has not only stopped my computer from picking up my new buddies (the virus boys) but it has made surfing a breeze. The browser loads quickly, the surfing is smooth and no problems to report yet *knock on wood*. So while change is hard to do, sometimes you have got to do it. I made the switch, and so far, it's been worth it. However, I am still looking forward to IE 7.....That will be fun, I'm sure....

Issue 109 – The Gung Ho Effect

I think we have all suffered from this troublesome itch that shows itself from time to time in our business. I call it the *Gung Ho Effect*.

Have you ever noticed the amount of effort and promotion that goes into a new program when it launches, only to have little or no effort being put forth a few months down the road? Sure, new owners are all excited and are spending money during the first few weeks of a launch, but then what?

You start to see the exchange less and less, while surfing. The owner seems to throw together *e-mails pleading* for members to surf more and to promote more. And then after a few more months, the exchange sometimes ends up offline, never to be heard from again. Some would say this is a good thing, as the proven programs with dedicated owners are all that's left, and I say....

The Gung Ho Effect is everywhere online! You don't have to be a program owner to suffer from it. One of the common misconceptions is that this business creates wealth in a few short weeks. The other misconception is that if you promote something every day for a few weeks, you can set it and forget it down the road. This happens to program owners, new affiliate marketers and people playing that horrible *slot machine marketing* game. It's time we all woke up!

You should be putting just as much effort into *your business* in 6 months that you are investing into it now. Remember a few issues ago, I talked about the slot machine marketing way of doing things, well the Gung Ho Effect is its nasty little cousin. This business takes time to grow. It does not happen overnight, but if you arm yourself with the knowledge, and pace yourself to be still growing in 6 months time, you will be in good shape.

It's a bad habit to get into and I hear it all the time in NetMarketingForum.com and in e-mails. If you are a new owner, stop relying on your members to promote your business. Start advertising! Affiliate marketers, do not jump ship in three months when you don't see the riches right away. Again, this business takes time to grow, the key is to keep that same level of dedication 6 months from now that you had when you first started online!

Issue 110 – Focus!

Focus your time and focus your energy! You've heard me ramble on and on about keeping the programs that you are promoting to a minimum. Here's something that goes along with this point and has proven to help me tremendously in my exchange campaigns.

Let's say you are promoting *Program X* and you have created a new splash page for it. So you start to promote *Program X* through your splash page and main affiliate link in the traffic exchanges. A good rule of thumb I use, is to promote my splash page at least 75% of the time, while my affiliate link gets the remaining 25%. Let's take it one step further.

You may not be content with the results that your splash page is generating so you decide to design 2 more to go along with the one in rotation. This gives you 4 sites to promote. 3 splash pages for *Program X* and then 1 affiliate link. Spread it out so that you still give 75% to your splash pages and be sure to **track** each splash page. See which of the three is pulling in the best number of click throughs and sign ups and you've got a winning formula.

After you have found out which of the three works best, use your rotator to insert the best performing splash page in place of the 2 that did not do so well. If you start seeing less results, try another 2 new designs and repeat. By tracking multiple splash pages, promoting the same program, you can effectively test and track the results of your designs any time you want.

Issue 111 – 80 / 20

Sometimes, I feel like the advice I find online flies under the radar. I have attended countless seminars, I have written dozens of articles and basically every reputable owner in this business has been preaching this simple but so very effective rule... Promote your business with splash pages! Again, this is not earth-shattering news, but I did a little test during my 3 week absence from H.E.N., and guess what I found out?

To this day, with every 'big name' traffic exchange user and owner on the planet preaching the importance of *proper* splash page advertising, only about 20% of the web sites in rotation at any given exchange are splashes. Yes, that means over 80% of the pages I see when surfing any given exchange are the same old generic affiliate pages that these program owners hope and pray that you promote endlessly.

I'm not sure what needs to be done so that this point gets across. I have written an entire training course on how to maximize your traffic exchange results. There have been a few well written e-books on the topic, but still, folks are trying to promote someone else's program with zero benefit to themselves.

Get yourself a splash page! Promote any business you want, but promote yourself in the process. If you do not know how to build a splash page, hire someone who does, join Quick Adz, or use the splash page creator from Traffic Tornado or Click Voyager, but for the good of your business, use splash pages!

The worst part is that these same people that choose to ignore the advice will be the ones in 3 months that throw their arms up in the air and scream that the exchanges are a waste of time... Want proof that this is so far from the truth? Check out the names of the people that do choose to use splash pages, and what do you see? You see people's names that have been doing this for years. Go with what works, grab yourself a splash page!

Issue 112 – Size Does Matter?

I did a small little study this past week on the number of traffic exchanges that are being promoted. Yes, I saw hundreds of programs while I surfed this past week and I wanted to share with you some points that I thought would help us better understand how important it is to promote your business in the traffic exchanges.

First of all, it makes complete sense that traffic exchanges are promoted in other traffic exchanges. Especially for newer programs, it seems logical to go after the customers you are looking for directly from the source! So of course, traffic exchanges are seen at every turn while you are surfing. Here's some things I noticed.

Without a doubt, the most popular exchange that I saw promoted this past week was 10KHits4UNow.com (I saw this program almost 50 times a day). Some people have mentioned to me that this promoted so heavily for all the benefits and bonuses that come along with securing a downline in this program. Bravo to them I say! This program also allows members to place their picture and name on all referral sites, so it's a bonus for both exchange and member.

Some other exchanges that I saw promoted heavily were TS25, Traffic Pods, Hit Harvester (more on this later), the Doug Williams exchanges, I Love Hits, Click Voyager, Traffic Roundup, StartXChange, Advertising Know How, Wolf Surfer, Hit2Hit, TrueViewTraffic and Hit Safari. Yes there were hundreds of others that I saw, so if you are an owner that promotes their own business, *good on ya'!*

What was very interesting is how much Hit Harvester was being promoted? I don't know about you, but don't you find it very difficult to find your referral URL in the HH member's area? I do know what it is, but it did take me quite some time. So one could argue that this program is being promoted heavily by the owners themselves. I'm sure it could be a referral link or two, but as an owner, I do know that Hit Harvester does spend money to advertise their program.

What is alarming, though, is the lack of real benefit to the referrer from the majority of these sites. Let's be honest, it's only recently that customized referral pages became the normal practice, so a big number of these sites I saw in rotation are generic referral pages. There was zero benefit to the user, so I'm not sure why they are promoting it so much?

Please excuse the length of this article, but I feel it's a very big issue in this business. Some of the bigger programs have relied exclusively on member support and promotion, which can explain why some of these programs are not as effective as before. Also, the newer traffic exchanges did not seem to be promoted that much at all, which does not surprise me, but does make me worried about the dedication behind some of these newer owners. It's really not rocket science, if you want more members in your traffic exchange, you need to promote it. Yes it costs money, yes it takes time, yes you may have to spend a few hundred dollars on advertising. This is after all a business, is it not?

All in all, my study proved a point I was trying to make. The more I seem to see certain traffic exchanges, the better they are performing. Take a look at any of my Top Ten lists during the past few months and not only will you see the same names on the list, you can be assured the programs are being seen in the other exchanges. So my advice to anyone still questioning what makes a traffic exchange great? I would argue that the more I see a traffic exchange being promoted, the most trust and faith I will put into it!

The size of the exchange does not matter as much as the dedication of the owner / members, in my opinion. But hey, that's just Jon's opinion...

Issue 114 – The Traffic Exchange Guy

I'm not sure what else we can do? I use 'we' to describe anyone that has ever discussed the importance of self-promotion. Or that has talked about the benefits of using splash pages. Maybe they did some seminars about how to effectively surf and use traffic exchanges. Why am I not sure what else to do? Simple, I surf these things for hours each and every day and guess what I see?

Affiliate pages!

75-85% of every web site I see is a generic affiliate page that some poor soul thinks is going to generate a referral. As blunt as I can be, please, for the sake of your precious time and money, stop promoting these pages. I have been over this so many times, but still *75-85%* choose to promote XYZ Affiliate site!

Grab yourself a few graphics by doing a search on Google, set up and design your own splash page. Upload your picture, stick your name everywhere you can, join a forum, but do not promote someone else's business without any benefit to your directly. Your most important asset in this business is your name. Use it to your advantage!

Hey, if you are not good at web design and do not know how to create a splash page, no need to worry. There are dozens of great services online that can help you out. For a small fee of between $15-$30, a professional can design a splash page for you. It could be worth much more to you in the long run, and if you could increase your awareness online by spending a minimal amount now, it's a lot easier to brand yourself down the road.

If anything, the message in this is to be pro active, not *re*active. Get the ball rolling and get yourself a splash page or two. The biggest problem facing this business is the attitude that traffic exchanges do not work. Why is there an attitude like such? Simple, people promote an affiliate page, put their time and effort into promoting it, and then 3 months down the road, have nothing to show for it. If you are promoting yourself as well as an affiliate program, you are doing your business a world of good. PLUS, combined with a splash page, you will be getting real results from your surfing!

I recently created a brand new service called TrafficExchangeGuy.com where I have begun to enroll clients into 'traffic exchange' education and training. It's the first of its kind of consulting service with one goal and one goal only, to get people results in this business. I've been at this for 6 years now, and I am so positive that 2006 will be a **huge** year for the exchanges. I hope you share the excitement many of us are feeling. Be sure to check out my new site if you have tried this business, but have not seen the results you expected.

Issue 115 – Three And It's Free?

"Refer 3 and break even!!!"

I am deeply concerned every time I see statements like that on ad copy throughout the net. These are the ones that tell you all you have to do is refer a handful of people and you too can 'break even'? What is wrong with that picture?

Have we decided that mediocrity is acceptable? Do we no longer want to *make money* and are we content with just getting by? I know I'm not. This attitude seems to plague a lot of the ad copy I have been reading while surfing the exchanges (yes, I *read* sites while surfing). And it's not from people's splash pages, this is from the ad copy of big name online marketing companies.

Now there is a big difference between aiming high and having unrealistic expectations. Becoming a millionaire by joining some MLM and expecting millions in a month, that is unrealistic. However, setting a goal of a six figure income in the next few years, is aiming high and putting a realistic goal for your online business.

We all know how hard it can be to refer 'just 3 and then it's free', so why not aim for more than that. Get out of the 'just getting by' mentality and really get your business off the ground! The tools are out there and the networking opportunities are there as well!

Issue 116 – The Year of the Auto Surf

"2006 - The Year of the Auto Surf Exchange!!!"

OK, disclaimer first. I have never been a fan of auto surf exchanges. I rarely use them, if ever and have even done my part to try to promote the benefits of manual surfs over the auto surfs, in countless issues of HEN.

Now that I've got that out of the way, let's state the obvious. Auto surf exchanges are immensely popular. These programs make manual surf exchanges look like guppies in an ocean. As much as it pains me to say it, the auto surf industry may be headed to bigger and better things in 2006.

Let's look at the numbers, while a decent sized manual traffic exchange has 5,000 members, a small auto surf program would have 20,000. When manual surfers complain about not seeing results (A.K.A. not using splash pages), the auto surfers *rave* about the money they make and the hands-free surfing they do. Is this a good thing?

I mean, I have my opinion, but I just cannot ignore the obvious. Auto surf programs are here and people love them. This does not mean I'm going to be surfing them or even promoting them, however, I think that 2006 will be a very good year for not only our little side of the industry, but for the auto surfs as well.

There is a lot of attention, outside of the traffic exchange industry, being focused on the auto surfs. And while the majority of it is not glorious publicity, it will be interesting to see what happens to them in 2006. Will they continue to grow? Or will they fade away? We'll see in a few months....

Jon's Note: 2006 was the year of the auto surf for all the wrong reasons. Do a search in Google for Storm Pay and 12 Daily Pro to find out all you ever wanted to know about these things.

Issue 117 – The Passion That Separates Us?

I find it very disturbing at times to be a traffic exchange owner and surfer. Not so much with the state of my businesses, but the attitude that seems to project from certain exchange owners and surfers. Simply put, they have no passion.

I used to do sales in an offline company, and the first thing you are taught is to be excited about the product you are selling. What are we selling? A product? A program? Your brand? You? So why are we so 'ho-hum' about our businesses?

I have a 5-year game plan, and this is how I see it. Without passion, these plans will crumble. Let's be honest, surfing for 6 hours a day to see zero results is very disheartening, so how do we remedy this? Simple, have some passion in your business and pride in your business models.

If you hear someone comment on how ineffective exchanges are, tell them to go get a splash page. If you are seeing little results, revisit your game plan and try new things. When you pour that first cup of coffee in the morning, get excited that you will make some sales today. It starts with you and the attitude you have in your business.

If we constantly feel sorry for ourselves and have a negative attitude about our business, guess what the outcome will be? However, if we put some passion into our business practices and have a game plan, there is really nothing that can stop you from reaching those goals. It works!

Issue 118 – It's Time For The Broken Record

Fair warning, what I am about to discuss is something I have gone over quite a few times. However, I think it's such an important topic that I need to go over it again. Here's something that should get everyone's attention right away...

Internet marketing is the only industry on this planet where profits are expected right away!

Look at a typical offline business, what is the turnaround target? 3 years? 5 years? How about a restaurant? 5 years for sure. So why is Internet marketing success required to take less time than a trip to the corner store? It amazes me, it baffles me, it sometimes even disgusts me.

Again and again, I cannot say this enough, it takes **years** to build a business. And that is a decent business, not a billion dollar empire. Let's be realistic. If you are looking at this as a hobby, guess what? Expect to wait even longer to see decent profits.

I cannot blame the folks that make up this interesting side of the industry. It's being bombarded everywhere you look. Autosurf for millions, forced matrix downlines, instant millionaire, and of course, let's not forget the new 'Rich Guru' knock offs. It's very hard to even begin to get into a business mind state with so much *bull* surrounding us.

So what can we do? I know this is not what many want to hear, but it's the sure-fire approach to building a successful Internet business. Are you ready for it? *Take your time!* Take your time with your advertising, spend more than one month promoting on XYZ Exchange. Do your research on the opportunity you are embracing, get to know your fellow networkers. Meet the owners, talk to them. Do not expect the world in 30 days or less.

I know it's not the *flashy dashy* answer that so many want to believe, however, it's the truth. It takes time, money and a whole lot of grunt work to build these businesses. Please don't give up after 60 days!

Issue 119 – Trend of the Month Club

The nature of the beast, that is what I call the very interesting things that happen every day online. From remarkable program launches, to simple support requests, this business keeps you on your toes.

The one thing that is certain is the ever-popular 'trend of the month'. Now by no means am I labelling all programs online as fads or scams or things you should avoid, but it's amazing to me how certain business models gather so much steam every few months and spawn countless clones and rip offs.

A few years ago, it was the 'bubble game'. I'm not sure exactly how these things became so popular, but the easy answer would be because they were 'fun'. Again, I'm not sure if anyone made a fortune by using them, but they spawned numerous clones. Fast forward to the randomizers, the doublers, the triplers, the auto investing sites and now it seems to be the pixel pages.

It will be very interesting to see how long these things last and sustain themselves, or if they are just a cash grab. I personally think these things will have a shelf life of about 3-4 months, but let's see in an April or May issue of H.E.N.

This business seems to breed a following trend like no other. No matter what happens, it's almost a guarantee there will be another program trend that pops up in a few months time.

I guess we should be wary of these things, but again, I will never say if they are legal or illegal. I'm not a lawyer and never claimed to be. I would beg for each and every reader of H.E.N. to please, use caution and do some research before you jump onto the latest and greatest!

Whatever you may think of them, they will be here next month and the next and the next....The question is in what shape and what form will they appear..

Issue 120 – 4 Points

I put this as the last issue of I Love Hits update, but I thought it is very relevant in this day and age of 'seeking immediate success' and the search for the almighty 'forced matrix millions'. I really hope you all enjoy it!

I call this little tidbit, my four keys to making long-term income online. It's not fancy, it's not flashy, it just works!

Number 1 - You Have To Spend Money! I know we have been bombarded with free offer after free offer, but whether it's an investment of time, or an investment with money, you have to 'invest'. This is a business, and a business cannot grow without some capital. Plus, if you are investing in your future, it makes sense to invest in your business.

Number 2 - You Have To Meet New People! It's time to put the 'network' back into this business. Case in point, in any industry on the planet, your networking skills will help you build a solid foundation for your business. Go to the forums, go to the seminars invest in an offline conference, use the phone, just get in front of as many people as you can. It makes a difference!

Number 3 - You Must Have Patience! On the Internet, we are told of instant riches, and success in 90 days or less. Forget about it. Remember, this is long-term income we want here, not a quick fifty bucks. You must have patience with your online business. This is the only industry on the planet where success is 'demanded' in weeks and months, not years. It just cannot happen, most offline businesses take 2-4 years to turn a profit, it should be no different online. Take your time, there is no rush!

Number 4 - The Dirty 4-Letter Word... Work! I know, I know... The images of sitting back with your feet up, sleeping in until noon, drinking pina coladas on the beach.... It's a myth! You must roll up your sleeves and put in work. Again, this is a business, it takes effort. Do not be scared of it, it's a very rewarding experience when you start to see returns for your hard work!

Take those four points as you wish, all I ever write about is what I have experienced. These things have worked for me, and trust me, I'm not a 'special person'. I was flipping pizzas only 4 short years ago, working on minimum wage. I did not plan on getting rich overnight and I did not give up my day job until I was certain I could supplement it. The Internet is a great way to earn a living... However, you have to earn it and that is what so many do not realize with an online business!

Issue 121 – The Death of the Splash Page

Could it be? I mean, many of us know that splash pages are one of the most effective tools online for using the traffic exchanges, so this may come as a shock to a lot of people, but please follow this article closely. Are splash pages losing their effectiveness?

I first used a splash page way back in 2002, in fact, we didn't even have a name for them then. Before that, all of the pages that were in rotation on the exchanges were generic affiliate sites. When I created my first splash, I wanted to stick out like a sore thumb. It was a very basic design, it had a big bold headline, and then a few words about what the viewer could gain by clicking on the link. You know how I knew I had something good when I created that splash page? My results soared, and I grew my business from using that one page for almost half a year!

I look back at why that splash page did so well for my advertising and it's simple, I stuck out. I grabbed people's attention quickly and got them to my call to action right away. This is a fundamental design of the pages that I see lacking these days, they are missing that uniqueness. There are so many cookie cutter programs out there and services that tell you they can create splash pages for you, but lack that simple 'attention grabber' that the first splash pages online had. This has to change.

Splash pages work, because they are different. Using a cookie cutter splash page is as effective as a generic affiliate link. However, with Splash Page Brander, a new tool developed this past week, things could turn around and bring 'uniqueness' back to the splash pages. Tools like this are essential for 'sticking out' from the clutter. What good is a call to action on a splash page, if no one reads that far down a splash to begin with. If you are designing your own splash pages, your attention grabber must be your primary concern.

Are splash pages dead? Have they lost their effectiveness? Yes and no. Yes, I think they are losing ground because they are more concerned about just 'being a splash page' rather than sticking out from the clutter. No, splash pages are here to stay and with tools like Splash Page Brander, the proof is that when used properly, they are the best way to brand yourself, your program, and to develop a strong presence in the traffic exchanges. Remember to stick out like a sore thumb, that is the power of the splash page!

Jon's Note: Splash Page Brander still exists and provides members with a great way to use E.S.A. (Exchange Specific Advertising). A new player named Kevin Anderson has joined in this movement as well with his very unique custom splash pages. The industry is maturing and creativity is becoming more evident.

Issue 123 – Being Told What To Promote

There was a recent debate in Net Marketing Forum about whether or not traffic exchange owners should be banning certain programs in their exchange. The debate brought valid points from both sides of the coin, but a survey by the owners of Vinterchange really captured my attention.

I was very shocked and concerned when the survey showed the majority of the members of this program wanted to be 'told' what was legal and what was not. In essence, they did not want to do the research themselves, they wanted others to find out for them. This got me thinking...

We are being taught to follow and not to lead. That is a huge problem with all online business, and I'm not saying for everyone to jump up, spend ten thousand dollars and develop their own program. However, for the good of your own business, stop listening to what people tell you to think and believe and find out for yourself. Develop your own opinions, develop your own presence, find out if the program you are promoting is legal by yourself, do your OWN due diligence.

Just because someone tells you a program is wonderful does not mean it does not require a good follow through in research. Check with other members, get feedback from various forums, ask questions, check out certain online consumer protection sites, but find out for yourself!

I really hope the people that answered that survey made a mistake and did not understand the question, because from what it looks like, we are putting our faith and trust for our own businesses into the hands of others. And not taking care of business ourselves...

Issue 124 – Traffic Exchange Brand Awareness

Everyone seems to be telling you that 'building a brand' is the thing to do. It's funny, because every few months there seems to be a new 'term' that strikes excitement into this business. A few months ago it was 'niche', before that was the famous taboo 'spam' term... Well, this month, it's branding, but what exactly is it?

The easiest way I can describe this is by asking a question. Have you ever heard of Coca Cola? Silly question, huh? But it's the perfect example of how powerful building a brand name is. It's advertising 101, it's what we should each be trying to do with our businesses. And by no means does this imply we need to become a multi-billion dollar empire like the folks down in Atlanta (Coca Cola), but the general idea is very sound.

It's simple, wherever you go, stick your name out there. Whether it be on a splash page, going to an online seminar, posting in a forum, adding content to a blog, make sure you are always being seen. Here's an example of something I heard this past week that struck me. According to a national advertising firm, every human being is bombarded with over 3000 advertising messages a day. 3000! Now how do you stick out from the crowd?

Hey, that's 3000 'everyday people'. We are traffic exchange surfers who more than likely get another 500-1000 ad messages put on top of the 3000 we already view. So what can you do to stick out? Simple, build your brand awareness. Build YOU! Everywhere you go, stick your name there. Yes, it takes time, it takes energy and it's not a glamorous task, but it works!

Maybe branding isn't the word we should be using, how about something similar, but adds our own 'flair' to traffic exchange advertising. Let's call it traffic exchange brand awareness.... Get people to know you using TEBA.

Issue 125 – Who Is On First?

More and more, people are talking about traffic exchanges, and for good reason, let's look at some tidbits I pulled from a few 'industry' publications this past week. One of these publications mentioned that within the next few years, nearly 40% of all Americans will work in some form at a home-based small business. Now, I'm not sure if this is the truth or not, but all indications points to more people looking at making money from home rather than from a typical 9 to 5.

What does this mean for the traffic exchanges? Well other than safe lists and the FFA programs, what other free or low cost advertising avenue is recommended to new people coming online to market their business? You guessed it, these little gems called traffic exchanges.

It's funny, because I used to argue with some of my colleagues during the past few years about the state of affairs in this industry. The main concern was whether or not any growth was taking place. So is growth happening in the exchanges? Are we all starting to see real good results from the exchanges? Well.... Yes!

More and more, TE Surfers are embracing the splash page concept as well as getting out of the habit of promoting a generic affiliate page. This is increasing awareness of the power of branding, *something we mentioned in an issue of HEN about 2 years ago* and more importantly, people are starting to promote themselves. A recent poll in NetmarektingForum.com showed that a huge percentage of the surfers either thought the TEs were at their peak or constantly improving. These are great signs!

I am extremely excited for this business, and even more for people that are coming on board and seeing the power of these programs firsthand. Surfers are wising up too, they are not putting up with the lack of support from some exchanges, they are demanding excellent return on their time surfed. Bravo!

It's only going up from here, folks. Within the next few years, traffic exchanges will be positioned to be that 'front line' that most new marketers reach when looking for free or low cost advertising. How important do you think it is for you now to know this, and act on it? Remember last week's article about brand awareness and getting your web sites seen for a sustained amount of time? You are in a great position to really make an impact. The future is now, and it looks like 'Click Here For Next Site'!

Issue 126 – Do You Use A Logo?

Branding, branding, branding! That seems to be the word of the week, as more and more people are starting to realize the power of using traffic exchanges to create a brand. It's funny, because this is something advertisers have been focusing on for years, but just recently the folks online are taking part in the fun-filled world of brand awareness (I like to call it Traffic Exchange Brand Awareness).

Creating a brand isn't as easy as pressing a few buttons and presto, instant brand name. This takes years and a lot of effort to create. So if you have not started yet, get to it. Remember, as 'popular' the term is we are NOT *marketing* in a traffic exchange, we are advertising and there is a difference. Branding is one of the most important aspects of advertising and to create a brand, you need a logo.

OK, let me re-phrase that. You do not need a logo, but it makes it a lot easier. A logo is what people will use to identify your business. Let's put it this way. Can you name me the fast food chain that has a logo shaped like big 'golden arches'? If you guessed McDonalds, you have just seen the power of using a logo to brand your business. We can use these exact same strategies to create brand awareness in the traffic exchanges.

I have tried very hard to use my logos to create visible brands in this business. Check out Doctor Traffic , SWAT Traffic and I Love Hits for examples of the logos I use.

My logos were the best investments I ever made in my business. Sure, getting the logos created is one thing, but the time to develop your name brand and create awareness does take effort. The logo could be the first piece in your advertising puzzle.

Some may argue the need for a logo, so I will simply use my favorite example here. I guess McDonalds, Pepsi, Coca Cola, Fed Ex, UPS and all the other billion dollar companies must know something that seems to work for them... Make your logo work for you!

Issue 127 – Do They Work?

I always get a kick out of going to a popular marketing forum and seeing this topic arise every few days...

Do traffic exchanges work?

The normal answers pop up like, 'I tried them for a week but nothing happened,' and my favorite, 'These programs are going to fail in a few months.' I enjoy it because it's what has been said about traffic exchanges since the day of Urgle.co.uk, *that's a really old traffic exchange*. So for 6 years now, traffic exchanges have not been working, the results are not what is promised and they will crumble in a few months.

OK, that's enough sarcasm for one day, but it brings up a really good point. If traffic exchanges were so 'bad', then why are they one of the most recommended free resources to advertise your web site? Did you know that these programs are positioned so well that they are the perfect first step for new marketers to learn about advertising online? Yes, I said it! We are *positioned* in the perfect place!

I attended an offline seminar this past week and was blown away at the amount of new people that are coming online to find additional income through an Internet business. There are hundreds if not thousands of new people looking for a way to promote their business for little or no cost every day. This is so exciting for me because no one can tell me there is 'no growth' in the traffic exchanges any more.

Take a look at the latest TE Challenge, where brand new programs are getting hundreds of new members every week. Even my own program, I Love Hits, has received thousands of new members this past month, and it's still growing in leaps and bounds!

We, traffic exchange surfers and owners, are sitting very pretty. Yes I am a TE cheerleader! In the next few years, get ready for these things to explode as more and more people jump online and try to advertise their business. Now what are we all doing to get ready for this growth? That.... Is a question only you can answer!

Issue 128 – Pay Attention

I read a great article by Tim Whiston on NetMarketingExposed.com and it really got me thinking about this crazy business we call traffic exchange advertising.

I mean, I understand the whole concept of finding something that works and duplicating it, that's great. I mean, companies have been doing this for years. Someone comes up with a great idea, and then imitators and duplicators flood the market with cookie cutter products.

Sure, you can make money taking other people's ideas, but why not build your own legacy? So my little rant this week is about the importance of innovation in this business. First example, the pixel pages. Remember the college kid in England who started the first one, he was an innovator, his name was Alex Tew. Can you name me the guy or gal that created the second pixel page? Or the third? Or even the 1500th?

It does come with business, but the message I'm trying to get across is to be different. Stick out from the crowd. You do not need to re-invent the wheel, but try to create something unique to you. Bring your own flair into your advertising campaigns.

Yes, the sad fact is, 95% or more of you that read this article will continue to surf the exchanges day in and day out, promoting a generic affiliate site, and then in 5 months, throw up your arms and say *'traffic exchanges don't work'*...

But for the rest of us, let's roll up our sleeves and start to innovate! You want to know how to start? Simple, join a forum, post in a blog, *pay attention to the pages in the exchanges*, attend a conference and build your network. You will be amazed at what your mind can come up with when you feed it the right stuff...

Issue 132 – Don't Wait! Take Action.

What are you waiting for? I mean, be honest. Is their some reason you have not exploded your business yet? Now this little rant is meant to be directed at exchange owners, but you can use the example for any business model as well.

So again, I ask. Why do you not have thousands of members in your business yet? Is there something you are waiting for? Some magic button that you press and it automatically creates a database of thousands?

Why is it that the same names seem to pop up when asked, *what traffic exchanges do you see the most while surfing* in the forums? What makes someone like Austin from Traffic Surfer different than Billy Bob from XYZ Exchange? I'm going to reveal something, and while it may not be that 'magic button' people are looking for, once you 'get it', you will understand.

You need to keep your business in front of people for as long and as often as you can!

That does NOT mean launch a new exchange, spend a few hundred on advertising and then give up a month later. That does not mean e-mail me about a new traffic exchange and never spend a dime on advertising. And it definitely does not mean wait for your members to promote your business.

I call it traffic exchange brand awareness, and it is the single biggest reason why Tony Tezak is known in this business for being a 'TE expert' while Jimmy Smith is just a generic affiliate ID number for a generic affiliate program. And how does this happen? How do you stick out from the crowd? Sustained advertising!

There is no magic button that gets you results, and no excuse as to why your traffic exchange should not be celebrating 2000 members or even 20,000. It just takes effort and a whole lot of advertising.

So the decision is yours really, maintain your business or explode it!

Issue 133 – Forums Can Be...Fun?

Many of you know Net Marketing Forum is one of the most popular online marketing forums around. This forum was created with one thing in mind, a place where no one would be told what they can and cannot say about online business. I was a member of many forums in the past that did not allow you to speak up on certain topics, thus NMF was created.

Now I'm the first to admit, the forum can get a little crazy at times, but I wanted to share with you the power of online forums and what they can do for your business.

It is a very good idea to have a presence in a marketing forum, and if you want to explode your traffic exchange results, Net Marketing Forum is a must! The movers and shakers of the traffic exchange industry frequent NMF daily and if you want to get your name known, check out these few tips on how to make a great impression in an online forum.

Introduce yourself first. Do not put any advertising in your posts, especially in your first 'welcome' to a forum! Introduce yourself, tell everyone you look forward to being a part of the community and then start your search!

Search for topics that interest you. An online forum can be overwhelming at times, but take your time and scan through recent topics. If you find something you want to comment on, PLEASE DO SO! One of the biggest problems people run into is becoming a part of the forum, but not being active! People need to see your name, and adding constructive comments to a discussion really gets your name out there.

Remember though, this is a forum with many people. So not everyone will agree with each other. If you get someone who disagrees with you, do not try to fight back. Take comments in a forum with a grain of salt. It is just business and nothing is ever personal. Don't worry, if it gets personal, I will remove the offending posts!

And finally, stay active and have fun! The more people see you, the more your name will get known. This also helps with your *Traffic Exchange Brand Awareness* by being active. Keep your name in front of people in the exchanges and online forums, you will see some great results!

Issue 134 – Contests? Yay!

I love contests, and I should get back into the swing of things at I Love Hits and start them up again. Recently, TS25 had a nice little contest that I just found out about a week ago. It was cool, lots of cash being given away and I actually won a few credits as well for being a 'super sponsor' and such.

Why are contests important? Let me put it this way, a properly promoted and unique contest does wonders for a traffic exchange, while a generic 'free credit' giveaway goes un-noticed by the masses.

I mean, of all the contests out there, how many did you really pay attention to and become active in? Which ones really stood out from the crowd? Basically, which ones did you participate in?

So what does it take for people to get on board and promote a TE during these contests. Simple, show me an active owner, and I'll show you an active membership. If the owner is in front of the public, promoting his / her brand, chances are that attitude is contagious and people will get on board. So it all starts from within.

Contest are a lot of fun, and I always look for a unique one to jump in on. But just like the TE business, it can get crowded!

Issue 135 – So You Wanna Build A Downline Huh?

I have heard years of advice on how to build a downline in a traffic exchange. I have even heard you shouldn't try to build a downline in a T.E. With so much out there and so much conflicting advice, what is the best way to tackle this issue that pops up from time to time.

Let's be honest, building a downline in each and every new traffic exchange that pops up would be crazy, but it would be equally as crazy to not jump on a new program by a reputable company such as Logiscape for example. It would be well worth it to build a downline there because just a few weeks of effort can really pay dividends in the long run.

The first thing you should do is decide whether or not a new T.E. is worth promoting. You can generally get a feel for how well a new T.E. will do simply by looking at the site design. Does it look professional? Does it have a logo? Do you know the owner? Is it a legal business model? Remember, there are over 2000 traffic exchanges online, but only about 20-40 of them produce decent results. Do your research on this new T.E. and see what the general feeling around the industry is about it.

Next, build a splash page specifically for this T.E. This is paramount in your efforts because you will stick out from the crowd if a lot of people start advertising it. I created many splash pages for new T.E.s I knew would be a hit. Take a look at some of the splash pages I created for Max Traffic Pro , Traffic Pods and Pro Traffic Shop. Each splash page, I use the logo so that people know which program I am promoting, but it's unique enough to grab people's attention.

And finally, monitor your results. Promoting a new T.E. can take up a lot of time and you should only spend a few weeks promoting it. After that, it will become a flooded market and then it's best to 'suggest' a T.E. in your mailing list and / or through a downline builder. However, that initial rush can really help build your team in a new traffic exchange. Again, it's very important to know if that new program will stand the test of time. So do research and find out which new program will become the 'next big thing' in the Traffic Exchange Industry!

Issue 136 – The PayPal Debate

Bobby Ivie from <u>FunnyFarmTraffic.com</u> woke up to a surprising little email a few days ago. Apparently, his Pay Pal account had been suspended for owning and operating an auto surf. That's fine and dandy, but for one problem, Funny Farm Traffic is a manual traffic exchange and has been online longer than most of those 'auto surf' programs in the first place. Thus began our little adventure this past week.

Pay Pal really scared a lot of owners this week because as much as we tried to differentiate ourselves from the auto surfing programs, we all got lumped into one big pot. After a few days, Bobby finally got his account restored and got a firsthand look at what Pay Pal expects from manual traffic exchange owners.

The meat of it is this: to be compliant with Pay Pal's Acceptable Use Policy, exchanges had to dump their referral credit earnings. What this means is that Pay Pal views the credits we give our multi-leveled downlines a monetary value. And this makes sense, because if you think about it, owners are selling the credits for cash, thus they have a value.

Next, was the wording on the sites. Red flags come up with the words surf, URL, and downline. Strange, but again this is what Pay Pal expects, so a lot of owners followed suit. I mean, honestly it doesn't seem to be too much to ask.

The problem comes back to the multi-leveled referral structure and how to approach this. Again, if you choose to use Pay Pal, you must adhere to their terms. But does this go against everything that the T.E.s started as? Does this really effect your earnings and or referral bonuses? Does it put more emphasis on building your own business rather than a T.E. owner? So many questions and what better place than to discuss it than at <u>Net Marketing Forum</u>. There are some great discussions going on, and when owners and surfers get together, good things happen. Check out the thread and make your voice heard!

And a special thanks goes to Bobby Ivie for having to go through this all. It was not fun, I'm sure, but you really helped a lot of us out! Thank you, sir!

Issue 138 – Stop Following, Start Leading!

Do you want to know the secret to all this Internet marketing mumbo jumbo? Want to know why some folks earn tens of thousands of dollars a month while you only put together scraps from time to time? Want to know the 'secret' that these so-called mentors keep from you so that YOU keep putting money in their pocket and continue to build their businesses?

The answer is an easy one! Stop making these people rich and become your own leader! These folks that tell you to follow systems and never stray from their outlined path are guaranteeing your failure. Do you want to know why? Because of the 100 or so people they bring into the system, only a few will have the guts and the smarts to step away from their 'system' and build their OWN businesses.

That does not mean you need to develop your own program, or even your own product. Your product should be YOU, and YOU should benefit from every action you do online. Here's a test, how much money is your 'leader' making online, and then how much are you earning? If it was so easy to duplicate as they say it is, you should be earning as much as they are, correct? I'm willing to bet that is not the case.

I know some folks will be angry by this article, and that's fine, I expect it. I have never been one to shy away from controversy, but let me make a suggestion to you. The next time they tell you to follow them down a path, stand up and develop your own mailing list, your own ideas and most important, develop yourself into a leader. It's not the easy way, and that is what they hope will scare you away, but it works. And so far, it's the only way I have found any success online, by promoting ME first!

Issue 139 – K.I.S.S.

Keep it simple! I think this is a major problem with not only splash page designs these days, but Internet business in general. Let's be honest, how much attention does someone give to a page in rotation? Not enough I'm sure, but even when they do, why do some folks try to make it so complicated?

I really feel traffic exchange promotions should keep it extremely simple. We should know what our potential customers are doing, they are surfing for credits, so let's do our best to stick out from the crowd and, most importantly, get our message across as quickly and painlessly as possible.

I hate to use the old 'K.I.S.S.' principle, but it does work. By keeping our splash pages and traffic exchange promotions simple, we allow for our brands to stick out. Remember, use these program to create brand awareness and build your mailing lists, this is the real power behind a traffic exchange. You do not need a small novel to do this. A quick loading splash page, with your name all over it does the trick!

Issue 141 – Self-Education

It seems like everyone is an expert and everyone knows everything! Let me let you in on a little secret, I spend a HUGE amount of money on self-education material and I'm always investing in learning new skills. Why? Simple, life is a learning experience and I want my business to grow. The only way that will happen is if I grow mentally as well

.

I sucked at school too. I was one of the class clowns that just got by in high school and college. It was not that I was dumb, I just could not care less about the square root of a billion and two. However, once I got involved with online business, I became a sponge!

It's such a small thing you can do, but it can pay you so much in the long run. I've got a list of 'must read' books, that I will be sharing in the near future, but the biggest thing you can do now is become that sponge and soak up the information that is out there.

Whether it's a new e-book, a home study course, online forums, offline events, you should live by this saying... 'Always be learning!' It really does expand your mind about business and not only does your business grow, but you do as well.

Issue 143 – Don't Let It Go To Waste

This is a huge pet peeve of mine. As you all well know, running and managing a successful traffic exchange does take some work. It's not as easy as set it and forget it, unlike some of the more 'popular' business models that can be found online. And this, I think, really effects how long a traffic exchange stays online.

Here's my beef. A new traffic exchange will launch and get a lot of support, months go by and the owner seems less interested in maintaining the program, and things start to go wrong. First, it's the lack of customer support, then comes the abusive sites in rotation and then before you know it, a very promising and popular traffic exchange has become another closed chapter in the traffic exchange world.

My advice? **Sell the program before you ruin it!** I know of plenty of would-be owners that are dying to find a new business opportunity, why let such a good thing go to waste? If you have no interest in running a traffic exchange, the first question I would have is why did you start one? However, the more important thing to mention is to PLEASE sell it or change ownership.

These programs are not supposed to be a free ride, and it takes a lot of effort to maintain them. Do the surfers a favor and don't ruin a good thing.

Issue 144 – What Makes You... You?

Branding! Ahh, this seems to be the word of the day, doesn't it? Every few months, there seems to be a new term or word that gets thrown around the Internet, and marketers from here to Australia scramble to learn everything about it. Remember 'niche'? Or how about 'unique traffic?' Well branding seems to be the word of the week so I thought I would explore it a bit in this week's *Deep Thoughts*.

Want to know why Jon Olson is considered an expert in the traffic exchange industry? Or have you ever heard of the name Tony Tezak for example? Or let's even look at it from an offline point of view, what restaurant do you think of when you think of 'the golden arches'? This is all branding and it's one of the most important aspects of advertising.

And that's what we are doing, right? We are advertising. We are advertising to build our brand and to bring awareness to our business and / or product. Folks, the traffic exchanges are one of the best places to do this and do it very effectively. So many people will run around in circles trying to build a business online without this one key aspect of advertising planned out, what is your brand?

The easy answer, the brand is you! You are unique, you are different, you have something people should hear. And there is no 'e-book' that will tell you this and certainly no 'product' that will help you realize it. The only way to discover what makes you unique is to find out for yourself.

This does not mean you have to become an expert in physics. This does not mean you have to have a PHD in medicine. All this means is that you have to stick out from the crowd. You have to create that image for your potential clients. People come to me for consulting because the name 'Jon Olson' is branded to traffic exchanges. This did not just happen. And trust me on this, anyone can build their own brand. The real trick to it is to discover it for yourself. And that can never be taught, it has to be realized!

Issue 145 – The Internet Marketing Gurus and the Traffic Exchanges

I always get a kick out of going to these offline events. As many of you know, I attended quite a few this past year with the most recent being Mike Filsaime's Internet Marketing Main Event. I enjoy meeting new people, networking with other like-minded individuals, and of course, getting Jon Atwood's and Pat Lovell's theories on life (after a few beers). It's a great time, and you do learn lots of new things to help your business.

That being said, the traffic exchanges are still this gray area when it comes to the other side of net marketing. Most of the gurus or whatever they want to be called this week, chalk traffic exchanges up as a waste of time. They basically say safe lists and TEs are not worth the time and effort. Of course, these are the same blokes that are trying to sell you on a 15-page sales letter, so naturally, TEs are not a good place to push these kind of sites.

In Baltimore, Mike Gartner of LinkCrews.com had a conversation with a fairly big name in the business. The 'big name' stated that he never used traffic exchanges and wouldn't even give them a second thought. I got a chuckle out of this because I remember this man's website being one of the most promoted sites in the TEs about 6 months ago. Funny, imagine that, I know of this guy because of the branding that he did in the TEs. But alas, they are useless according to the powers that be.

So while some of the big names in the net marketing business won't be using TEs, I have got to thank people like Mark Joyner, Mike Filsaime and Gary Ambrose for not only owning their own traffic exchange in one form or another, but still saying that TEs serve a purpose and can be very effective when used properly.

Yup, I'm still waving the TE banner proudly!

Issue 146 – Jon Olson, Bah Humbug!

Did you know that I get more hate mail directed at my Top 10 list than anything I have ever written about in the past 3 years of Hit Exchange News? Why is it such a hot topic each and every week? Why do some traffic exchange owners HATE me because of this list? Simple, it's my opinion!

You see, the Top 10 list is comprised of the traffic exchange I FEEL performed the best for me that week. I don't just look at numbers, I take into mind everything from number of new subscribers I received, to whether or not the owner provided any valuable updates to its members. There is absolutely NO science to it at all, it's just my opinion on which programs I feel delivered the best results for me that week. Guess what, it won't be the same Top 10 in your campaigns because you are not Jon Olson, and you are not promoting the same things I am. My point is this, results will vary!

It's been a fun few years of running this newsletter and I wish I could share with you some of the lovely mail I have received because I did not list Top Surfer number 1 this week. It's crazy, but alas, my opinion. Honestly, no 'ranking' system can ever be THE WORD in this business, simply because different people surf and promote different things. What works well for you, may not for me.

My advice? Track your own results and develop your own Top 10 list that works FOR YOU! If you are interested in learning how to track your results and develop your own Top 10 list, contact me.

Issue 147 – Thank Goodness For TrafficRoundup

Thank Goodness For Traffic Roundup

Stephen and Bobby from <u>TrafficRoundup.com</u> sent the most important email update that this traffic exchange industry has ever seen and I could not do an issue of Hit Exchange News without mentioning it and discussing the importance of it.

I have been saying this for years, and finally someone has the stats to prove me right. In a recent poll from Roundup members, it was asked, "How long have you been involved with TrafficRoundup?" Here is the stat that sticks out for me:

19.20% of the membership answered, 'I am brand new.'

Wow! What does this tell us? Why is this such a huge chunk of marketing information that every single one of us can use? Simple, it shows that there are hundreds of people joining these programs every day and that the bulk of who you should be promoting to is new members to the traffic exchange industry.

These programs have been the front line for years, and finally we can prove it. New people join the traffic exchanges for free and low cost advertising, these are the perfect potential clients you are looking for. Imagine being the first person they meet about how to make money online? Imagine you are the first person that teaches them how to develop a winning strategy to build your mailing list? This is exactly the position you want to be in.

So the numbers are there, the proof is known, now what are you going to do about it? How are you going to develop your strategies to best utilize this information? Think of some creative ways you can develop some campaigns that attract this huge chunk of the market, and you are on your way to traffic exchange success.

Issue 148 – Free vs. Pro

So it's been an interesting few weeks for the pro only traffic exchange model. As many of you know, I used to co-own one of the last true pro only traffic exchanges on the net and it was a great endeavor. One of, if not the most profitable joint venture I took part in.

Fast forward to today and you can see the extremely popular launch of Click N Putt, which has become not only a very good pro only program, but a successful traffic exchange as well. So one could argue, the pro only model is alive and well.

Flip the coin and you see, RoyalSurf.com and TrafficExchangeBusiness.com switching gears to become free-to-join traffic programs. So on this side of the coin, one would argue the strength of the industry is in the free programs.

My take is this (as it always has been). They are simply two options. Neither one is 'stronger' in features or deliver better results. I get great results from both models, they are just two different options for achieving the same thing, getting hits to your web sites.

The topic has been discussed for months and whatever side of the coin you are on, I do really think when programs launch like Click N Putt, and re-launch like Royal Surf, there is room for both models!

Issue 149 – The Timer

5-4-3-2-1... Next site! When the traffic exchanges started, the industry standard countdown timer was at 30 seconds. Ask someone to wait 30 seconds to click on the next site these days and you are bound to hear moans and groans. Yes folks, the timer has shrunk...

So do we need a 30-second timer? Do we need something like a minute ,perhaps? Or is the new standard of 15 seconds a good target? Here's my take, and I know it will ruffle some feathers. I like short timers.

Now, I think the minimum should be 10 seconds. And no more or less than that because we should be encouraging people to use traffic exchange friendly pages (ie. splash pages) in their promotions. We do not need a half a minute to view a graphic, short paragraph and a call to action. A good splash page should get your message across in 3 seconds or less.

As for results, I get better results from the programs with 10, 15 and 20-second timers, rather than the older 30-second timers, so the argument for me that a longer timer is a better quality page view, doesn't stand up. *Note: This is from my results only, you may get better results than me at a 30-second timer. Track your own stats to be sure!*

Who knows what the future of the 'timer' will be. Maybe even an exchange without a timer? Maybe a 5-minute timer? Or maybe we should keep it like it is. Say yes to 10-15-20-second timers. Say yes to results!

Issue 150 – Finally!

It's funny, because the number one question that comes up time and time again in both online forums and live seminars is, 'How do I get results from the traffic exchanges?' Why is this funny? Well, the information is out there yet only a handful of people use it. There are forums, seminars, e-books, tutorials and so much amazing information out there, yet only a few people seem to put this into action.

Action. That is the word of the week! It's fine to get all this information, but it's useless unless you take action. For example, have you seen the 'Kevin Anderson invasion'? Take a look at what this gentleman is doing and you can see someone who is putting a lot of that useful information into action. His splash pages grab your attention, the exchanges are getting flooded with his programs and his name is getting out there. This is exactly what everyone should be doing, make your impact felt!

It does not take thousands of dollars, it just takes some creativity, some elbow grease and persistence. Do you have your splash page rotated in the exchanges? How well would you compare it to some of the other splash pages you have seen? Are you taking part in forum discussions? How about attending online seminars? Have you networked with other exchange owners? What are **you doing** to build your business?

Issue 151 – The 5% Rule?

You've heard it a million times online. 95% of the people will fail in online business. Only 5% will make a good living from their online endeavors. Where do they come up with this stuff? I mean, where are all these stats coming from?

Seeing that we're in the business of throwing around numbers, I have a feeling it's even less than 5%. Let's say it's 2%...How did I come up with 2%? Well, out of 100 traffic exchanges online, only about 2 of them are worth using. *gasp*. I can hear the jaws dropping around the industry, but let's look at just a few of the garbage programs that are out there. I can think of about 200 or so 'investment surfs' and heavens knows, we don't need to scratch that wound.

I just think about 2% of the people in this business treat it like a business. And no, that does not mean your 'hobby' cannot be treated as a business either. A hobby can turn into a business, I'm a perfect example of that. However, the one thing I did once I saw the growth potential was this, I re-invested my earnings into promoting and developing my 'hobby'.

So 5% will succeed? I guess so. I for one think I'm in the 95%, because if I get comfortable and tell myself I have 'made it', then my business will not grow. One of my mentors told me something once that has stuck with me for years and I will quote him here:

"When people get comfortable, they get lazy. And when people get lazy, they cannot move forward. Being comfortable is the quickest way to stop progress!" - Kenneth W. Olson (My father – One of the best teachers I have ever had!)

Issue 152 – Scammy Scam Scams

What is a scam? And why are they everywhere online? Two questions, multiple answers, but to this day it boggles my mind when I read things like this:

I lost money in this program after they shut their doors, oh well...

Or even...

One of these programs will finally make me rich, I just need to keep joining them until I find the right program...

I called it slot machine marketing a few years ago and essentially, it's not getting any better. People still come online and pull that handle, hoping the next program they join will make them rich. Rich huh?

Someone let me know when those yachts will be ready because I'm still trying to figure out how to 'get rich online'. LOL. I don't know if it's sad or funny, or a little of both, to see these people continue to go through these programs day in and day out. I mean, what will it take for folks to finally realize (get ready for this) that making money online is *actual work*!

Oh, the scams are everywhere! They will continue to exist as long as people play the game of slot machine marketing. Here's a tip, and even though it's THE most used phrase online, it doesn't hurt to hear it again...

If it sounds too good to be true, it is!

Issue 156 – The Real Bad Advice Syndrome

I just finished reading an update from a fair-sized traffic exchange and I was shocked at some of the advice that was put forth in the update. It mentioned things like 'do not use splash pages to brand your name and picture' and even worse, don't advertise yourself in the Top 10 / Top 40 traffic exchange lists.

If you are NOT branding your name and getting it known throughout the Internet, you are wasting your time and putting money in someone else's pocket. Be sure anything you do, especially with traffic exchanges, benefits you in some way or form. For example, if you are promoting GDI, make sure 'Joe Smith' is promoted just as much as GDI. Keep your name in front of people.

The other shocker was to avoid promoting in the bigger and better performing exchanges online. This made me very concerned for newer exchange users that would have read that and promoted their tail off in an exchange with 300 members. This is not proper time management for your advertising efforts. And it is NOT effective. Here's a little tip that Mike Paetzold mentioned in one of his seminars recently...

In the established exchanges, promote to build your brand, in newer exchanges promote to sustain your brand.

Essentially, this means to keep your face / name in front of everyone around the industry. But with hundreds of new members joining the larger exchanges every week, you hit a larger market to build your business. But also be sure to keep it visible in the smaller exchanges to remind folks that you are still there.

This is advice that is proven to work. This is how I run my businesses, this is how I make my living online. It's not easy, and it's not 'silver spoon fed', but it works... if you work it.

Issue 157 – Log In To Activate...No Problem!

You know the messages, *Please log into your account or else it will become in-active*. I have no problem with these at all, in fact, both of my exchanges use that same tactic to get more active surfers. It makes sense, if you sign up for a program, use it and be sure to get everything you can out of it.

Here's my problem though. How can you expect people to be active in your program when a few things never happen;

1. We never see your traffic exchange when we surf. Out of sight, out of mind.

2. You never send weekly or monthly updates.

3. Our credit bank has hundreds of credits and you are delivering about 10 hits per day.

Why on earth do you expect people to use your program when these three *extremely simple* management tasks have not been taken care of. I myself refuse to surf at a traffic exchange that does not deliver what I can surf in a day. For example, if I surf 20 sites, give me my 10 page views (given it's a 2:1 ratio). That's the least a traffic exchange can do for its members, but it's rare.

Want to know one of the biggest factors I have in listing my Top 10 list each and every week. Take a look at those 3 points I listed above. Those programs listed have at least 2 if not all 3 points taken care of. (Logiscape rarely sends updates, but they take care of point 1 and 3 VERY well).

So this is my opinion... Don't send me the 'activate account' emails when you are running your traffic exchange into the ground!

Issue 158 – I Am A Traffic Exchange

I am a traffic exchange. Some people may call me a start page exchange, a hit exchange or even a click through program. Sure, I have many names, but I really am a simple tool to use. Sometimes, I think people make me out to be more complicated than I am. I have been around since the late 90s and am finally starting to make my mark online.

I deliver traffic to people's web sites. People get me confused with many other forms of online advertising. I am not a safe list, I am not a search engine, I am not a free for all link exchange and I **am not** an auto surf investment scam.

It has been said I would not last for more than 3 years. I even had some of my owners say I wasn't good enough to be a player in the Internet marketing industry. Actually, come to think about it, I still do. Yes, some big name owners still do not view me as a legitimate online advertising resource... Talk about self-hate, huh?

I provide my members with page views to their web sites at a very steady pace. I sometimes think people give up on me too quickly, mainly because they have a slot machine mindset when it comes to building a business online. Don't worry, I'll still be here when you come back to me in 6 months.

I need my surfers, and value them very much. Without surfers, I am nothing. Without splash pages, I am nothing. Without ad tracking, I am nothing. And without a positive attitude, I am... Nothing. I am a traffic exchange, and I thank you for sticking with me for the past 7-8 years.

Issue 159 – Jon's Best of List For 2006

Warning: I know most folks that are familiar with H.E.N. will recognize this statement... These are my opinions **only**. The following list is my opinions of the best and sometimes 'newsworthy' traffic exchanges of the past 12 months. Enjoy it, I had a blast putting this together.

Best Traffic Exchange of 2006: TS25.com - Week after week, this program delivered the results. Yeah, Logiscape will never be known for their stunning customer support, but you cannot deny the impact and results that this exchange delivers. The best and still champ in my opinion!

Best Traffic Flow: This is a tough one because like all things in this business, it varied from week to week. But for constantly always being able to deliver traffic, the award for best Flow of 2006 goes to HitSafari.com

Best Features:StartXChange.com without a shadow of a doubt. Tim Linden, the owner, constantly improves this traffic exchange with user friendly services, cool little features and he always seems to be promoting 'user activity'. One of the most unique scripts and fun traffic exchanges to surf.

Best Upgrade: MaxTrafficPro.com wins this award. Now it's hard to measure what makes the 'best upgrade', but MTP delivers on so many levels. It's affordable, it delivers and the traffic flow is very steady. Combine that with an owner that is always improving the program and you've got the recipe for some great return on your investment.

Most Fun To Surf: You mean other than the two I own? LOL. Just kidding. This award goes to MysticalMaze.com One of the original 'game surfs', the Maze is not only a great traffic exchange, but it always keeps people wanting more with its simple yet highly addictive 'maze game'.

Surfer of the Year: I have got to give credit to each and every person that has ever clicked 'next site' in any traffic exchange this past year, but one name sticks out simply because he 'branded' himself before anyone even thought of the idea. And yes, Tony Tezak has officially retired, but he was still a huge impact surfer this past year. So again, enjoy your retirement, Tony. I hope everyone learned lots about promoting themselves first from your examples.

Owner(s) of the Year: So many amazing folks in this business, such a tough decision. I know I'll catch some heat for this, but I have to give it to two of my 'close associates'. Am I playing favorites? Maybe, but this is my opinion. Robert Puddy and Rich Taylor. These guys put together the Focus 4 Seminar series last year and guess what? The traffic exchange owners came out in droves! The people that attended the seminars got to learn firsthand what traffic exchanges were all about and for that reason, I don't think anyone else has done more for our industry than these two guys.

So there's my little list. Like I said, it was a lot of fun to put it together. I hoped you enjoyed it and all the best in 2007 to each and every traffic exchange surfer and owner!

Issue 160 – The Community

As many of you may have read in past issues of Hit Exchange News, I follow a theory that I came up with called *Traffic Exchange Brand Awareness*. The general idea behind this is to keep your name / program in front of people in the exchanges for the long run. To look at results on a month by month basis, rather than day by day.

This is accomplished, of course, by keeping your site rotation in the exchanges, but how else can it be done? By becoming a vocal and active member of the traffic exchange community! This means to not only keep your site around for all to see, but to use your **real name** when coming to online seminars, online forums and tele conferences. This is a trick that not everyone will feel comfortable with, and that's fine, but you can have that extra step by providing people with your name. It's a trust issue and this is so important online.

Like I mentioned, coming to the online forums helps tremendously. Sure, it's good to sit back and soak up all the information, but voicing an opinion and continuing to be a voice in the industry will help. Online seminars too, I can remember almost each and every member who has attended my seminars during the past 3 months, simply because they use a real name and come each and every week.

Building your online presence in the traffic exchanges is more than just 'clicking'. It takes time. It takes effort, but is well worth it in the long run.

Issue 161 – Help Me...Please!

I've got a major concern when it comes to traffic exchanges and the lack of customer support that exists. I mean, don't get me wrong, sometimes I mess up and miss emails / phone calls, etc., however, the chances are you can get a hold of me if you try. Support is one thing, but when you offer support and make it more complicated than it needs to be, you miss the boat too. Here's what I mean.

The new thing seems to get these help desk programs installed. These only exist to frustrate customers. Have you ever tried to 'set up a ticket'? You need to register for this silly little ticketing system, which is completely separate from the registration you used to get into the program in the first place. This is not customer service, this is brushing people off.

I know, I will hear the garbage about how much time it saves, yadda yadda yadda. Sure, it may save the program owner time, but what about the customer (remember them?) who wants the answer as quickly as possible.

I detest ticketing systems and it's the number one reason I will never get one on my traffic exchanges. I know I am only one person, but maybe instead of force feeding your members a 'help desk', why not ask them first what they want? I'm willing to bet they will say they want answers quickly... Hmmm, I mean we could always give out a phone number for support too... But that would mean people would get help right away... Hmmm...

Issue 162 – What's In A Price?

I got a very interesting email today from Savvy Clicks. They are changing the prices for the credit packages, but actually lowering them. This exchange seems to be around the industry average of $10 for 1000 hits. But what about the prices at Traffic Roundup? Or the prices at TS25? Is there an average? Why do companies charge what they charge?

It's amazing to see the pricing structures of different traffic exchanges. Take for example, the upgrade at Link Crews. 40 bucks a month! This is a very bold price point when you can upgrade at a program TS25 for 25 bucks a month (Platinum level). Take it even lower though, and you see upgrades for 10 dollars per month like an I Love Hits upgrade or 5 dollars a month for a StartXchange upgrade. It goes to show the diverse set of business people we have running the traffic exchanges.

So what does a credit cost? I mean what is the value because Traffic Roundup offers 1000 credits for only $6.95, but Traffic Swarm charges roughly $20 for 1000. Same traffic, same people surfing. HUGE mark ups by some companies.

This does come back to tracking, and whatever programs work for you are obviously the ones to support and purchase from, but again, it's remarkable to see how different companies in the exact same industry price their products. A big thing that makes you go hmmmmm...

Issue 163 – What Exchanges Should You Upgrade In?

I get this question asked a lot, so I thought I would break down a few areas that I look at when choosing a program to spend money on and upgrade. Here they are:

1. I know some folks wouldn't put this as the first area to look at, but I do, and that is who owns the program. Have I worked with this person before? Do we have a business relationship? Have I had good experiences with this owner? There is so many things that can be said about who owns a program and how well it will be received by the industry.

2. Results / Traffic Flow. Plain and simple. If a traffic exchange delivers what it says it will, I will upgrade. If I'm seeing good returns on my time in the program, it's a good bet to upgrade.

3. Site Design / Theme. Does this look like an out of the box stock script? Or has the owner invested into getting custom work done to the script and to the site design. You can tell a lot about the longevity of a program by its looks.

4. Gut Feeling. Never ever second guess your inner voice. If you have a good feeling about a program and you think it's a winner, it will be. If something sounds too good to be true, it is. Your inner voice never lies.

5. Value. Are you getting a good bang for your buck? Is the price of the upgrade a good value? Is the owner charging way too much? You must get good value for your upgrades. Check what comes with your upgrade and make sure it's at or above industry standards.

Those are my tips on choosing a solid traffic exchange to spend your money in. If the program delivers on those points, you can be sure you are making a wise investment.

Issue 164 – Too Many Exchanges?

It's remarkable how this industry operates. A few years ago, you could count the number of exchanges that existed on two hands. Then came the boom, we had thousands of them. About a year ago, it slowed down again as new exchanges were launched few and far between. However, this year we seem to be moving towards an increase in new programs. Is this a bad thing? Are there too many programs online?

Yes and no. Yes, I think there are too many to surf. It's become a challenge to remember which exchanges you want to use every day simply because of the choices out there. Owners are doing a very good job at launching these programs and gone are the days of 'free credits to sign up'. Thus, traffic flow usually has a head start out of the gate. However, the cream will always rise to the top.

And that's the big reason I say there will never be 'too many' exchanges because the programs that do well and continue to grow will be the ones where the owner invests his or her time, effort and money into it. Simply put, the best exchanges managed by the best people will always do well.

So sure there is a new wave of exchanges being launched, but this tells me that more and more people believe in the traffic exchange model. Owners are starting to learn and implement some great ways to bring people into their program, and this benefits everyone in the long run.

Remember, the cream will rise to the top!

The Future of the Traffic Exchanges

It's a great time to be involved with this industry. As you have read, things are not always rosy and peachy in this business. However, something I want to stress is that no matter how many times I have heard that these programs will not exist in a year, how 'un-targeted the traffic is', or how many freebie seekers exist in the exchanges, they continue to grow.

Why is that? It's simple. Traffic Exchanges are the front line. We do an amazing job of catering to the newbie. When someone hears they can make money online, the first thing they are told that they need to do is to generate traffic. I can only speak for myself, but when I got started, I looked for the free and low costs avenues of web site promotion. This is where traffic exchanges rule the roost.

While safe lists and FFA programs have their place, no other form of free advertising has grown so much than the exchanges. Sure, there are other ways to promote a business or web site, and I'm sure there are more effective ways to do it. But pound for pound, if you use them right and embrace the tools and services that work, traffic exchanges are hard to beat.

I always say there are two things that these programs should be used for, and only two. The first is to build that almighty mailing list or contact list. Everyone that is involved in online business will tell you that the 'money is in the list' and it's so true. Traffic exchanges are perfect for this.

The second thing is to build your brand awareness. Plain and simple. Promote YOU! And keep it in front of people for the long run. I call it traffic exchange brand awareness and it works.

So what does the future hold? More growth. With innovative programs and creative owners appearing every day in this business, I see great things ahead. More emphasis will be placed on branding and creative advertising. Exchange specific advertising will become much more of a factor and the interaction between surfer and advertiser will be stronger than ever.

Hits, clicks and misses. We've seen the misses, and hopefully we can learn from them. We can develop a strong industry with more owners and surfers working together. This is just the beginning, even if the industry is almost a decade old. We're young, but we are growing up fast!

It's not a job, it's an adventure!

Credits

This book, my career and my growth as a person could not have been achieved without the help, guidance and support from the following.

First and foremost, God! I thank you each and every day for the blessings you continue to show me. Thank you so very much for your gift of life and all that you have created.

My family: to my son, Matthew, you are the reason Daddy spends hours on end in front of this computer. I am trying to give you the best life I can and you are my reason for being. Thank you for bringing me to life!

My mom, you have been the best friend I have ever had. Your constant patience with me reminds me each and every day how important it is to stop and appreciate what really matters most.

My father, there is something you taught me a few years back that made the difference in my life. You told me there is no real wealth in working for someone else. I finally understand that when you said that, you meant fulfilment in one's personal life. Thank you for showing me how to 'finally' stand on my own two feet!

Kym, you stuck with me throughout the roughest of times. I remember $5 weeks in Toronto, living off of Kool Aid, Kraft Dinner and tuna. Thank you for being the best mother Matthew could ask for! I wish you nothing but happiness and success in your life.

My grandparents, thank you for your guidance, love and lessons. You are such wonderful people. My aunts, uncles, cousins and relatives. The island of Newfoundland for giving me my soul.

Blair, Dan, Bruce, Kevin, Matt, Luis, Kevon, Greg, Anthony, Dave, Hasahn, Mike, Kevin, Ossa, Jayne, Tanya, Nadine, Carla, Jessica, Deanne, Henry, Gabe and everyone that has ever stopped by 115 Main Street South. You guys are incredible people and kept me going for years on end!

Rich, Robert, Steve, Mike, Paul, Jon, Pat, UA, William, Bill, Cat, Brett, Dan, Tim, Michael, Eva, Jack, Aaron, Gary, Tony, Soren, Suzette, Nathy, Radouane and the hundreds of amazing people I have had the pleasure of meeting through the years all directly from my involvement with the traffic exchanges!

And finally, to each and every I Love Hits, Doctor Traffic, SWAT Traffic, Hit Exchange Survival Kit, Hit Exchange 101, Traffic Exchange Guy, Hit Exchange News, and Net Marketing Forum member and customer... You are all the reason I am in business. Without you all, I would be just another guy flipping pizzas. Thank you for putting your trust in my businesses, my vision and my dreams!

www.ingramcontent.com/pod-product-compliance
Lightning Source LLC
Chambersburg PA
CBHW051243050326
40689CB00007B/1048